On the Beaten Path
BEGINNING DRUMSET COURSE
An Inspiring Method to Playing the Drums, Guided by the Legends

LEVEL 2

RICH LACKOWSKI

Alfred Music Publishing Co., Inc.
P.O. Box 10003
Van Nuys, CA 91410-0003
alfred.com

Copyright © MMX by Alfred Music Publishing Co., Inc.
All rights reserved. Printed in USA.

No part of this book shall be reproduced, arranged, adapted, recorded, publicly performed, stored in a retrieval system, or transmitted by any means without written permission from the publisher. In order to comply with copyright laws, please apply for such written permission and/or license by contacting the publisher at alfred.com/permissions.

ISBN-10: 0-7390-7034-7
ISBN-13: 978-0-7390-7034-5

Cover Photos: Drumsets © Larry Lytle • Drumset provided courtesy of DW/PDP
Other photos: Art Blakey © Time & Life Pictures/Getty Images / Robert Parent • Jeff Hamilton © Redferns / Clayton Call •
Al Jackson, Jr. © Getty Images / Michael Ochs • "Philly" Joe Jones © Getty Images / Robert Abbott Sengstacke •
Steve Jordan © Redferns / Clayton Call • Chris Layton © Redferns / Clayton Call • Mitch Mitchell © Getty Images / Michael Ochs •
Buddy Rich © Lissa Wales / www.drumpics.com • Max Roach © Lee Tanner/The Jazz Image • Ringo Starr © T. Eagan

 Alfred Cares. Contents printed on 100% recycled paper.

CONTENTS

	PAGE	CD TRACK
The Path	4	
Acknowledgements	5	
Reading Music Notation—What You Should Already Know	6	
Basic Blues and Shuffle Beats	8	
"Red House" from The Jimi Hendrix Experience's *Are You Experienced* (1997 remastered version)	8	1
"You Shook Me" from Led Zeppelin's *Led Zeppelin* (1969)	9	2
"Paying the Cost to Be the Boss" from B.B. King's *Complete Collection* (2008, single version originally released in 1968)	10	3
"Sweet Home Chicago" from The Blues Brothers' *The Blues Brothers Soundtrack* (1980)	11	4
"Revolution" from The Beatles' *1967–1970 (The Blue Album)* (1973, originally released in 1968 as the B-side to the "Hey Jude" single)	12	5
"Bad to the Bone" from George Thorogood & The Destroyers' *Bad to the Bone* (1982)	13	6
"Who Do You Love" from George Thorogood & The Destroyers' *Move It On Over* (1978)	13	7
"Boom, Boom" from John Lee Hooker's *Urban Blues* (1967)	15	8
"I Want to Be Loved #2" from Muddy Waters' *Hard Again* (1977)	16	9
"Manish Boy" from Muddy Waters' *Hard Again* (1977)	17	10
"Green Onions" from Booker T. & the MG's *Green Onions* (1962)	18	11
"At Last" (ex. 1) from Etta James's *At Last* (1961)	19	12
"At Last" (ex. 2) from Etta James's *At Last* (1961)	20	13
"Texas Flood" from Stevie Ray Vaughan and Double Trouble's *Texas Flood* (1983)	21	14
"Pride and Joy" from Stevie Ray Vaughan and Double Trouble's *Texas Flood* (1983)	22	15
"Move It On Over" from George Thorogood & The Destroyers' *Move It On Over* (1978)	23	16
Basic Blues and Shuffle Fills	24	
"You Shook Me" from Led Zeppelin's *Led Zeppelin* (1969)	24	17–18
"Bad to the Bone" from George Thorogood & The Destroyers' *Bad to the Bone* (1982)	25	19–20
"Texas Flood" from Stevie Ray Vaughan and Double Trouble's *Texas Flood* (1983)	25	21–22
"Sweet Home Chicago" (ex. 1) from The Blues Brothers' *The Blues Brothers Soundtrack* (1980)	26	23–24
"Sweet Home Chicago" (ex. 2) from The Blues Brothers' *The Blues Brothers Soundtrack* (1980)	27	25–26
"Stone Crazy" from Buddy Guy's *Buddy's Blues* (1997, single originally released in 1962)	27	27–28
"Pride and Joy" from Stevie Ray Vaughan and Double Trouble's *Texas Flood* (1983)	28	29
"Red House" (ex. 1) from The Jimi Hendrix Experience's *Are You Experienced* (1997 remastered version)	29	30–31
"Red House" (ex. 2) from The Jimi Hendrix Experience's *Are You Experienced* (1997 remastered version)	30	32

	PAGE	CD TRACK

Basic Jazz Beats 31

    "Everybody Loves Somebody" from Dean Martin's *Dream with Dean* (1964) 31 33

    "What a Wonderful World" from Louis Armstrong's *All Time Greatest Hits*
(song originally recorded in 1968) 31 34

    "I've Got You Under My Skin" from Michael Bublé's *It's Time* (2005) 32 35

    "Theme from New York, New York" from Frank Sinatra's *Trilogy: Past Present
and Future* (1980) 33 36

    "Straight, No Chaser" from Miles Davis's *Milestones* (1958) 33 37

    "In a Mellow Tone" from Duke Ellington's *Best of Duke Ellington*
(song originally recorded in 1939) 34 38

    "In the Mood" from The Glenn Miller Orchestra's *Best of Glenn Miller*
(song originally recorded in 1939) 34 39

    "Chelsea Bridge" from Buddy Rich's *The Best of Buddy Rich (Pacific Jazz)*
(1997, song originally recorded in 1970) 35 40

    "Blues Walk" from Lou Donaldson's *Blues Walk* (1958) 36 41

    "The Sidewinder" from Lee Morgan's *The Sidewinder* (1964) 36 42

    "Moanin'" from Art Blakey & the Jazz Messengers' *Moanin'* (1958) 38 43

    "So What" from Miles Davis's *Kind of Blue* (1959) 39 44

    "Jeru" from Miles Davis's *Birth of the Cool* (1949) 40 45

Basic Jazz Fills 42

    "In Walked Bud" from Thelonious Monk's *The Very Best*
(2005, single originally recorded in 1947) 42 46–47

    "I've Got You Under My Skin" (ex. 1) from Michael Bublé's *It's Time* (2005) 42 48–49

    "I've Got You Under My Skin" (ex. 2) from Michael Bublé's *It's Time* (2005) 43 50–51

    "I've Got You Under My Skin" (ex. 3) from Michael Bublé's *It's Time* (2005) 44 52–53

    "Theme from New York, New York" from Frank Sinatra's *Trilogy:
Past Present and Future* (1980) 44 54–55

    "Moanin'" from Art Blakey & the Jazz Messengers' *Moanin'* (1958) 45 56–58

    "In Walked Bud" from Thelonious Monk's *The Very Best*
(2005, single originally released in 1947) 46 59–60

    "Everybody Loves Somebody" (ex. 1) from the Dean Martin's *Dream with Dean* (1964) 46 61–62

    "Everybody Loves Somebody" (ex. 2) from the Dean Martin's *Dream with Dean* (1964) 47 63

CD audio examples performed by Rich Lackowski.
Instructional photos by Larry Lytle.

THE PATH

This book picks up where *On the Beaten Path: Beginning Drumset Course, Level 1* leaves off. It is designed to help you get "on the beaten path," that is, to help you play the beats and solos that our mighty drumming predecessors play on the songs we love. You will learn everything you need to know to go from the first thought of "I want to play the drums" to playing some of the most legendary beats and solos ever recorded! Many books claim to do this very thing, but what sets this book apart from the rest is that here, you will learn by playing along with the greatest drummers in the world—all types of famous drummers from a variety of musical styles—and you'll learn how to play the beats that they perform on some of the most famous songs ever recorded. This book explains what these drummers play on their songs by breaking it down in a way that gets you to learn to read music and start developing your own ideas into beats, fills, and solos.

I believe that drummers learn by mimicking their heroes. Sure, beats grow and change and morph into original ideas, but all drummers—from aspiring beginners to seasoned professionals—are naturally inspired by what other drummers are playing. The proof is in all those people you've seen air drumming along to some key part in a song. Many of these people have never sat behind a drumset or even held a drumstick, but the drum beat and the framework of the song somehow gets them to raise their arms in the air and act out their interpretation of a moving drum passage. It's basic human instinct. When writing this book, I wanted to guide this natural instinct in a way that logically feeds you information as you need it so you can accelerate the process of learning how to play your drumming heroes' beats.

I know when I first started playing the drums, even though I had just begun taking group lessons on the snare drum in school, that the *real* learning happened when I got home and threw down my boring class snare drum book that our teacher assigned to us. I put on the headphones each day, sat behind my drum kit, and tried to mimic the beats and fills that the drummers were playing on my favorite songs. Through trial and error, I was eventually able to play the songs and at least fake my way through the more difficult parts.

In this book, I will accelerate this process of trial and error, and guide you through the things that every drummer needs to know in order to play the drums. This book can be used with or without a teacher. Although you don't *need* a teacher to use this book, it would benefit you to go find a drum teacher in your area and take lessons. A teacher will get you to practice if nothing else, but they will also correct any bad techniques you may be developing before they become hard-to-break habits.

Now let's get started and begin our journey On the Beaten Path!

Icons Used in This Book

The following icons are used throughout this book to help you learn valuable information and to become a better drummer.

 **TIP:** This icon is shown near helpful tidbits of advice.

 **TOOL:** This icon is shown near key concepts or tools that will help you play the drums with more expression and personality.

 **TERM:** This icon is shown near explanations of key music notations and concepts.

ACKNOWLEDGEMENTS

I'd like to thank everyone who helped bring this book to fruition. I am extremely grateful for each and every contribution, no matter how small, and your help is sincerely appreciated. Without your encouragement and support, this book would never have been possible.

I dedicate this book to my parents, Bob and Mary Jean, who helped me take the first steps down my drumming path. When I showed an interest in playing the drums, you were there to help me. When I needed a teacher, you hooked me up with one of the best around. And when I needed some encouragement, you were there supporting me every step of the way. Thank you for your patience as you listened to me fumble through the first several years of rushed fills, the repetitive beats that I played a zillion times, and my shortcomings when I didn't have even a faint concept of what it meant to groove. You helped empower what became a life-long passion and I thank you from the bottom of my heart for giving me that opportunity.

I also dedicate this book to my sisters, Janet and Chris; and my brothers-in-law, Sam and Scott, who each encouraged me to write my own path regardless of how difficult it may have been at times; and to the love of my life, my wonderful wife Nikki Lackowski, a constant source of love and encouragement, and an amazing woman who never stops believing in me or my talents.

Thanks to my friends and everyone that I've ever had the privilege of making music with, including Nikki O'Neill, Josh "Cartier" Cutsinger, Jon Sfondilis, Matt Hannon, Chris Moseman, Matt Lapperre, Tish Ciravolo, Ron Manus, Tommy Norton, Harold Branch, Jedd Scher, Cale Reese, Mark Ruppe, Paul Stabler, Todd Janko, and so many others who have embarked on various musical journeys with me. And thanks to every drummer mentioned in this book, and countless others who have inspired me to pick up the sticks and play the greatest instrument in the world.

A very special thanks to Ron Manus, a dear friend and a fun mentor; John O'Reilly Jr., Link Harnsberger, Holly Fraser, Mark Burgess, Kate Westin, Ted Engelbart, Glyn Dryhurst, Dave Black, Gwen Bailey-Harbour, Antonio Ferranti, Mike Finkelstein, Daniel Frohnen, Samantha Ordoñez, Ann Miranda, and the entire team at Alfred Music Publishing; Neil Larrivee and Mark Wessels at Vic Firth; Steve Lobmeier, Trish Johnson, Jim Bailey, Michael Robinson and all the wonderful people at Evans Drumheads; Don Lombardi, Juels Thomas, and Scott Donnell at DW Drums; John DeChristopher and Sarah Malaney at Zildjian; Frank Corniola and all the wonderful people at *Drumscene*; all the great folks at *Modern Drummer*; Phil Hood, Andy Doerschuk, and the folks at *DRUM!*; everyone at *Drumhead*, *Drummer*, *Rhythm*, and *Percussioni* magazines; Bernhard Castiglioni at Drummerworld.com; Mike Dolbear at MikeDolbear.com; Tiger Bill Meligari at TigerBill.com; Bart Elliott at DrummerCafe.com; Martin Osborne at Onlinedrummer.com; John Coia at Drum.com; Bob Gatzen; all the readers of *Modern Drummer* magazine and the readers of *DRUM!* magazine who voted for *On the Beaten Path: The Drummer's Guide to Musical Styles and the Legends Who Defined Them* as the "No. 1 Educational Book" in both of their 2008 Reader's Polls and who voted for *On the Beaten Path: Progressive Rock* among the winners in both of their 2009 Reader's Polls; and to Dean Turner, my first drum teacher who led me on my first steps down the beaten path. I thank you all from the bottom of my heart.

—Rich Lackowski

READING MUSIC NOTATION—WHAT YOU SHOULD ALREADY KNOW

If you have completed *On the Beaten Path: Beginning Drumset Course, Level 1*, you know the following things about playing the drums.

The Basics

Parts of a drumset, setting up the drums, holding the drumsticks, basic hand technique, basic foot technique, parts of a drum, tuning the drums, drumhead selection, drumstick selection, playing basic rock beats and fills, flams, and drags.

Measures

Music notes are shown on a group of lines and spaces called a *staff*, which is divided into sections called *measures*.

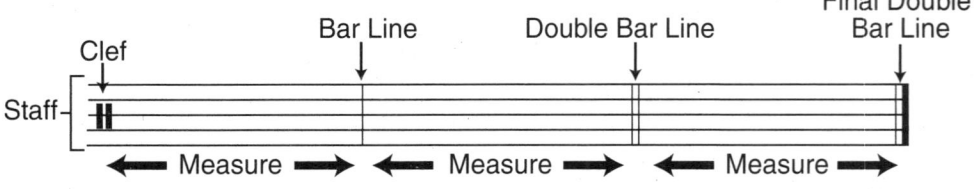

Bar lines indicate where measures begin and end. *Double bar lines* indicate a section break, like moving from a verse to a chorus in a song. *Final double bar lines* indicate the end of a piece.

At the beginning of each staff of music, there is a *clef sign*, which indicates how the music should be read. Unpitched percussion music typically uses the *neutral clef* (𝄥).

A *repeat sign* has two dots before a final double bar line (:|) and indicates going back to the opposite-facing repeat sign (|:). If no opposite-facing repeat sign is present, repeat from the beginning of the music.

Notes and Rests

The duration of musical sounds (how long or short they are) is indicated by using different types of *notes*. Corresponding symbols called *rests* are used to indicate silence.

Notes are used to indicate musical sounds. Some notes are long and others are short.

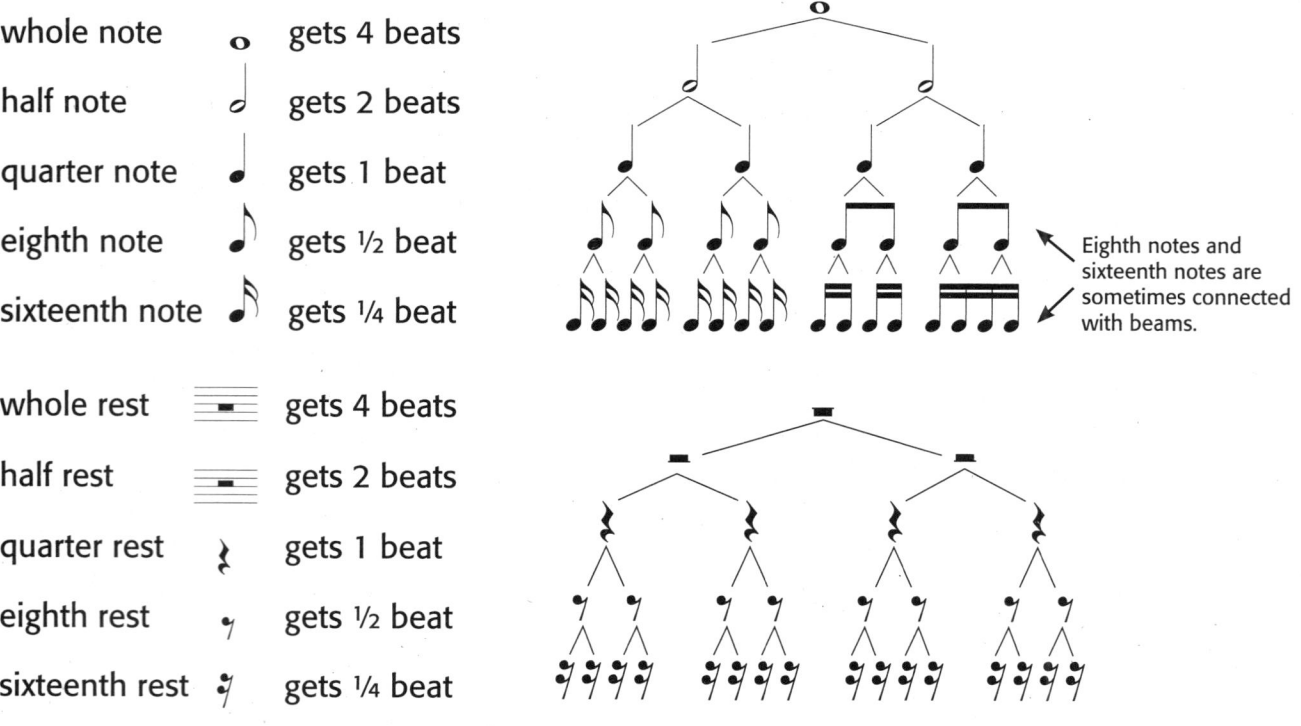

whole note — gets 4 beats
half note — gets 2 beats
quarter note — gets 1 beat
eighth note — gets ½ beat
sixteenth note — gets ¼ beat

whole rest — gets 4 beats
half rest — gets 2 beats
quarter rest — gets 1 beat
eighth rest — gets ½ beat
sixteenth rest — gets ¼ beat

Eighth notes and sixteenth notes are sometimes connected with beams.

When a dot follows a note, the length of the note is longer by one half of the note's original length.

dotted half note   𝅗𝅥.   gets 3 beats

dotted quarter note   ♩.   gets 1½ beats

dotted eighth note   ♪.   gets ¾ beat

A triplet is a group of three notes played in the time of two notes of the same value. Triplets are identified by a small numeral 3 over the note group.

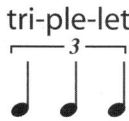

Time Signatures

A *time signature*, a symbol with two numbers, is placed at the beginning of a piece of music to indicate how the music is counted:
4   The top number shows the number of *beats* (or *counts*) in each measure, in this case, four.
4   The bottom number shows what kind of note gets one beat, in this case, a quarter note (♩).

In 4/4 time, a whole note receives four beats.

A half note receives two beats.

A quarter note receives one beat.

An eighth note receives half of a beat.

A sixteenth note receives a quarter of a beat.

You will encounter other time signatures as well, which follow the same rules. For example, 12/8 indicates that there are 12 beats per measure, with an eighth note getting one beat.

Tempo

Tempo is the speed of a musical piece or passage. Tempo is indicated by a musical term or by an exact *metronome marking*. A *metronome* is a device that clicks or flashes lights to indicate the tempo. For example, ♩ = 120 means the metronome will click 120 times per minute, and each click represents a quarter note.

Drum Notation

Each line and space of the staff designates a particular drum or cymbal.

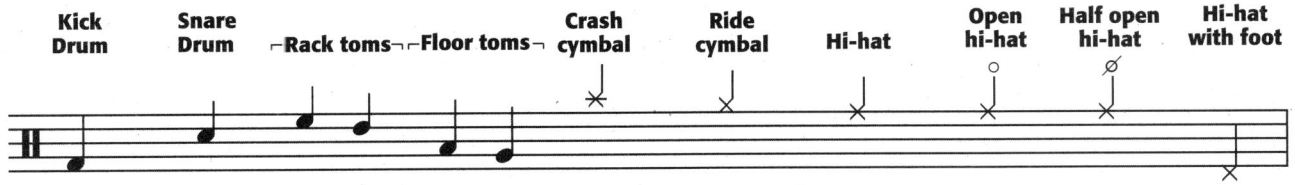

BASIC BLUES AND SHUFFLE BEATS

"Red House"
FROM THE JIMI HENDRIX EXPERIENCE'S *ARE YOU EXPERIENCED* (1997 REMASTERED VERSION)

Much of early rock 'n' roll was rooted in the blues, and this classic song by Jimi Hendrix is a great example of a blues tune with a good, solid blues drum beat, beautifully played by the late great Mitch Mitchell. The tune is from the album *Are You Experienced*, which VH1 named the 5th greatest album of all time and *Rolling Stone* magazine ranked no. 15 on their "500 Greatest Albums of All Time" list. This song was originally omitted on the USA version of the 1967 release, but fortunately made its way onto the 1997 U.S. remastered edition.

Original transcription (0:16):

Track 1

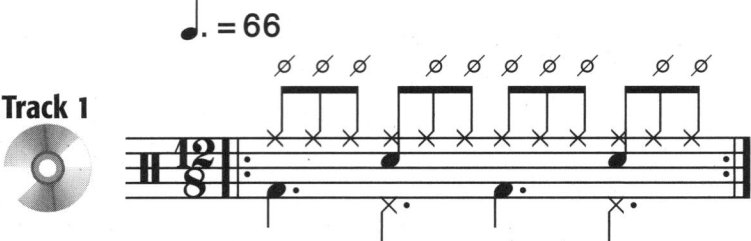

This tune is in $\frac{12}{8}$ which means there are 12 beats per measure and the eighth note gets the count. Let's start by playing eighth notes on the hi-hat with your right hand to the pulse of the music. Start by counting along with each hit:

1–2–3–**4**–5–6–**7**–8–9–**10**–11–12 | **1**–2–3–**4**–5–6–**7**–8–9–**10**–11–12

and so on. The circles with the slashes through them that are above the hi-hat notes indicate that the hi-hats should be played slightly open so that they have a "sloshy" type of sound. Let's give it a try!

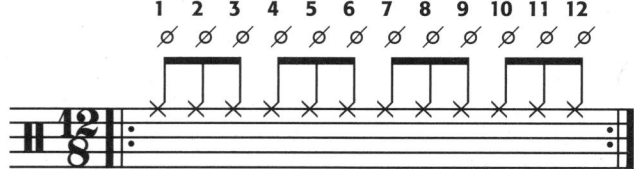

Next, let's add a kick drum hit on beats 1 and 7. Start slowly, and gradually increase the tempo as you feel comfortable.

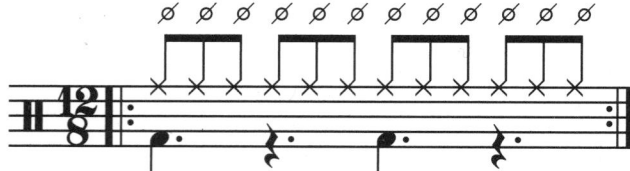

Now, let's add a snare drum hit with your left hand on beats 4 and 10.

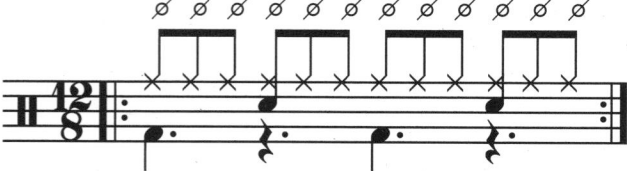

Finally, close the hi-hat on beats 4 and 7 by stepping on the hi-hat pedal with your foot, and you'll be playing the blues just like Mitch Mitchell does on the recording.

Congratulations! You just learned to play your first blues beat!

BASIC BLUES AND SHUFFLE BEATS

Mitchell mastered the delicate balance of keeping the groove fluid, yet solid, while simultaneously packing in his share of solos and fills around Jimi Hendrix's guitar. The result was an extremely complementary chemistry in musicianship, where the dynamics and emotional impact of the songs were greatly intensified. Mitchell played the drums on every Jimi Hendrix Experience recording and he was Jimi's longest-running and most important creative partner.

"You Shook Me"
FROM LED ZEPPELIN'S *LED ZEPPELIN* (1969)

John Bonham lays down a nice heavy blues beat in this legendary tune from Led Zeppelin's debut album. Notice that this groove, like the previous one, is in $\frac{12}{8}$. This is a very standard time signature for many blues songs and something you'll see a lot more of as you continue to play the blues.

Original transcription (0:05):

Let's start by playing the beat we just learned in "Red House," but this time, let's play it a little slower, and with the hi-hats fully closed.

Next, let's remove some of the hits on the hi-hat. For this example, just play the hi-hat on beats 1, 3, 4, 6, 7, 9, 10, and 12. Listen to the way Bonham plays it on the recording and mimic along.

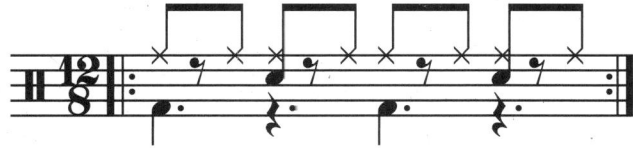

10 BASIC BLUES AND SHUFFLE BEATS

Now, add kick drum hits on beats 3 and 9.

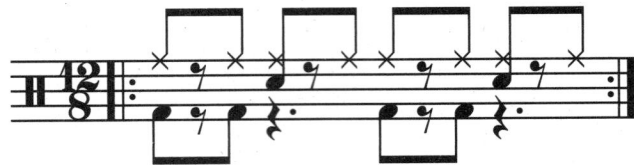

Finally, add some more kick drum hits, this time on beats 6 and 12, and you'll be playing the deep powerful blues groove just like John Bonham plays with Led Zeppelin!

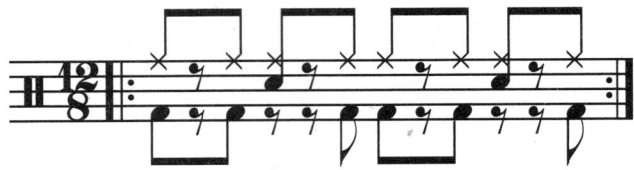

"Paying the Cost to Be the Boss"
FROM B.B. KING'S *COMPLETE COLLECTION* (2008, SINGLE VERSION ORIGINALLY RELEASED IN 1968)

This tune by B.B. King, one of the greatest bluesmen of all time, features the shuffle beat. This is an important beat that you'll encounter many times as you continue to play the drums, and it's the cornerstone of many blues and early rock tunes. Listen closely to how drummer Sonny Freeman plays this beat, and then give it a try yourself!

Original transcription (Intro):

Track 3

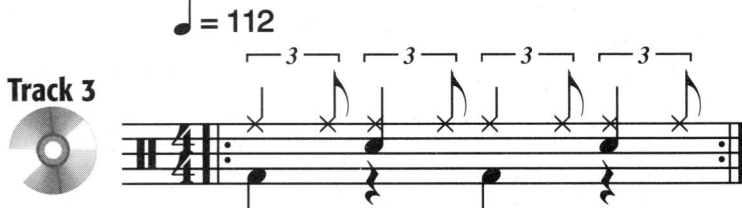

Notice that this beat is a bit similar to "You Shook Me," except it's played faster and, in this example, there are a few less kick drum hits. In general, it is easier and more common for slower blues grooves like "Red House" and "You Shook Me" to be written and played in 12/8 and for faster blues/shuffle grooves like "Paying the Cost to Be the Boss" to be written and played in 4/4. There are several ways you'll see this shuffle beat written, so, to prepare you for these situations, the most common notations are listed here. Remember that, even though the way the beat is notated varies, the actual shuffle beat is played the same in all cases.

A

BASIC BLUES AND SHUFFLE BEATS 11

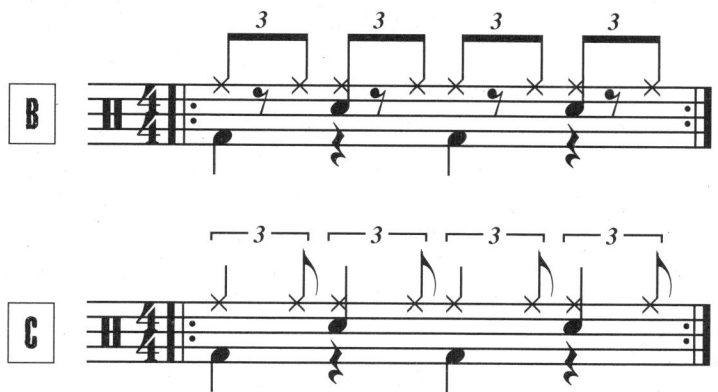

$\boxed{A} = \boxed{B} = \boxed{C}$

Throughout this book, we'll notate these types of shuffle grooves like you see it in the example below, which is based on triplets. Now go ahead and play the shuffle beat. Start slowly, and gradually increase the tempo until you can play along with the recording.

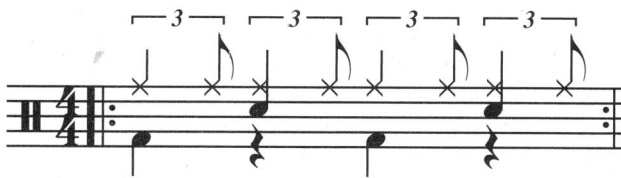

"Sweet Home Chicago"
FROM THE BLUES BROTHERS' *THE BLUES BROTHERS SOUNDTRACK* (1980)

This blues standard features another shuffle beat, sometimes called a shuffle with "four on the floor," which refers to the kick drum being played on all four beats. This shuffle beat, masterfully performed by drummer Steve Jordan, is similar to "Paying the Cost to Be the Boss," but "Sweet Home Chicago" is played a bit faster and a bit more driving with "four on the floor." Give it a try! Like the previous beats, it's best to master the groove slowly and then gradually increase the tempo until you can play along with the original recording.

Original transcription (0:07):

Track 4

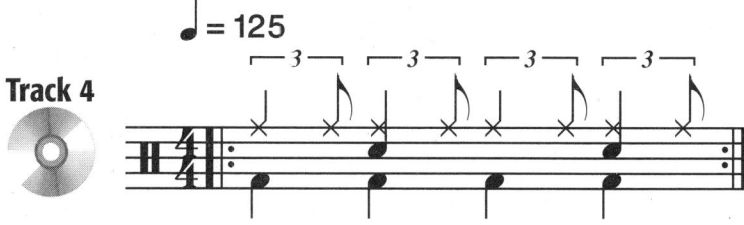

"Revolution"
FROM THE BEATLES' *1967-1970 (THE BLUE ALBUM)* (1973, ORIGINALLY RELEASED IN 1968 AS THE B-SIDE TO THE "HEY JUDE" SINGLE)

So far, our hands have been busy playing the bouncy shuffle beats on the hi-hat. Let's give our hands a rest and try playing the bouncy shuffle beat with our foot instead. Although this song is not often attributed to being in the blues genre, the drum beat masterfully performed by Ringo Starr has a definite blues shuffle quality to it, and it's a great groove to get that kick drum foot in shape!

Start by playing this very slowly, and gradually increase the tempo as you feel comfortable. If any of your muscles start to cramp up, reduce the tempo and try to relax as you play the groove. Try to make your limbs flow in a relaxed motion instead of forcing everything.

Original transcription (0:08):

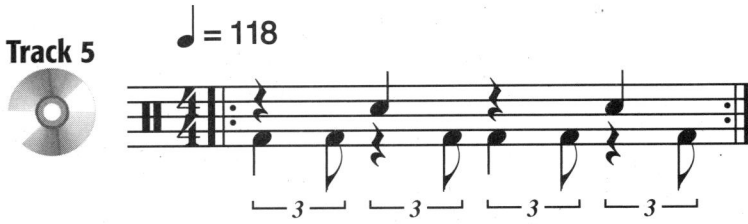

Track 5

Remember to keep breathing! Some people have the bad habit of holding their breath when they play more difficult passages. This just deprives your muscles of oxygen, which is vital to keep them from cramping up. Breathe!

RINGO STARR

In addition to being the drummer in The Beatles, the greatest and most influential band of all-time, Ringo was also a great innovator. He was the leading pioneer that broke rock music out of the jazz/swing-rooted styles commonly found in the music of Chuck Berry, Elvis Presley, and Little Richard, and he was one of the first drummers to popularize performing on a drum riser, playing with matched grip, and tuning his drums low and using muffling techniques.

"Bad to the Bone"
FROM GEORGE THOROGOOD & THE DESTROYERS' *BAD TO THE BONE* (1982)

This tune features a drum beat, played on the recording by Jeff Simon, that's very similar to what we just played on "Revolution," but "Bad to the Bone" is a bit slower and adds triplets on the hi-hats. Start slowly, and increase the speed only after you've mastered the drum beat at a slower tempo.

Original transcription (0:08):

Track 6

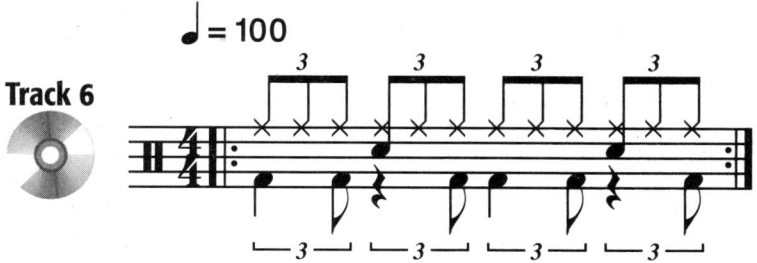

Accented Notes

An *accented note* is played louder than the other notes around it. When notated, an accented note looks like this:

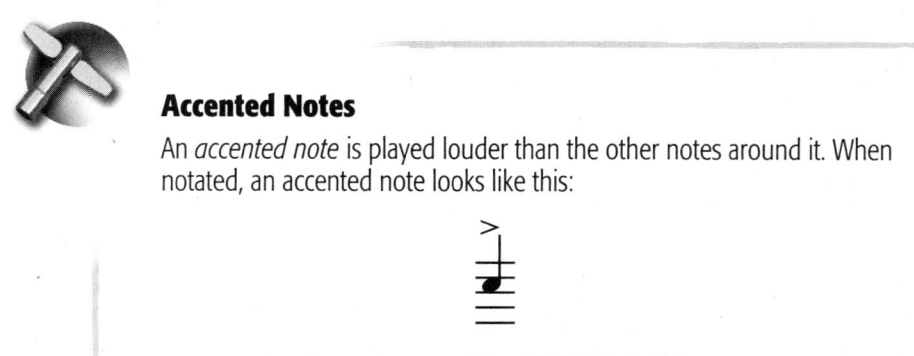

"Who Do You Love"
FROM GEORGE THOROGOOD & THE DESTROYERS' *MOVE IT ON OVER* (1978)

Although slow $\frac{12}{8}$ beats and quicker shuffle beats are commonly featured in blues tunes, there are plenty of other ways for drummers to play the blues. This tune features an accented floor tom groove that creates a drum beat quite different than any of the beats we've learned so far.

Original transcription (0:04):

Track 7

Start by playing quarter notes with your foot on the hi-hat.

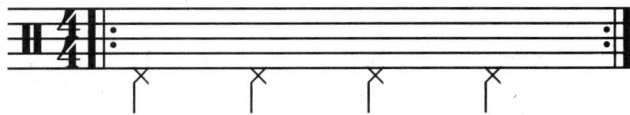

14 BASIC BLUES AND SHUFFLE BEATS

Next, play the following pattern on the floor tom while playing quarter notes on the hi-hat with your foot. Pay attention to the indicated sticking. These hits on the floor tom lock in tightly with the tune, so listen and play along.

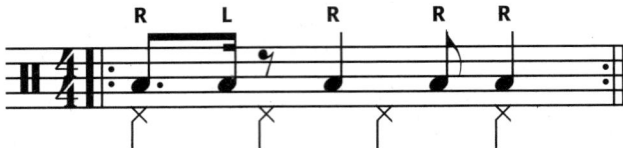

Now, add the following floor tom hits, again paying special attention to the indicated sticking.

Next, let's add a few more floor tom hits, again paying special attention to the indicated sticking.

Let's play it again with all of the floor tom hits.

Finally, play it with accents on the indicated beats. These accents lock in tightly with the tune, so listen and play along. Practice this beat until you can play it smoothly and comfortably.

BASIC BLUES AND SHUFFLE BEATS

"Boom, Boom"
FROM JOHN LEE HOOKER'S *URBAN BLUES* (1967)

This classic tune by one of the greatest blues legends of all time features another beat that doesn't fall into the traditional categories of slow $\frac{12}{8}$ grooves or the faster shuffle beats that make up so much of blues music. Drummer Al Duncan crafted this drum beat, which perfectly fits the rhythm and attitude of the song.

Original transcription (Intro):

Track 8

Let's begin by playing the hi-hat and the kick drum on beats 2, 3, and 4 of the first measure, and on beat 1 of the second measure.

Next, let's add snare hits on beats 3 and 4 of the first measure, and on beat 1 of the second measure.

Finally, add a snare hit on the "let" of the triplet that starts on beat 1, and you'll be playing the drum beat just like it was played on this classic blues track.

16 BASIC BLUES AND SHUFFLE BEATS

Drummer for Muddy Waters for nearly two decades, Willie Smith appears on all of Waters's Grammy award-winning albums, including *Hard Again*, *I'm Ready*, *They Call Me Muddy Waters*, *Muddy "Mississippi" Waters Live*, *The London Muddy Waters Sessions*, and *The Muddy Waters Woodstock Album*. Smith is one of the pillars of blues drumming, and a true legend of the instrument.

"I Want to Be Loved #2"
FROM MUDDY WATERS' *HARD AGAIN* (1977)

Drummer Willie Smith integrates a short triplet drum fill right into the drum beat of this song, which was written by the mighty bluesman Willie Dixon, and performed here by "the father of Chicago blues," Muddy Waters.

Original transcription (Intro):

Let's start by getting comfortable playing the basic blues beat before adding the triplet snare fills.

Now, let's add that triplet fill that comes at the end of the two-bar phrase, beginning on the "let" of beat 3 in bar 2.

BASIC BLUES AND SHUFFLE BEATS 17

Finally, set up the song by playing a triplet on the snare starting on beat 4, before launching into beat 1 of the repeating two-bar drum groove.

"Manish Boy"
FROM MUDDY WATERS' *HARD AGAIN* (1977)

The true essence of the blues is wonderfully captured on this recording by Muddy Waters. Muddy begins the tune with a *call and response* between his voice and his guitar. Call and response describes a sequence of two musical phrases where the second phrase is an artistic imitation or reflection of the first musical phrase. Waters makes the call with his voice—"oh yeah"—and the response with his guitar while other musicians and spectators holler out their enthusiastic praise before Muddy unleashes his excited and authoritative "Wooooooo!" that cues the rest of the band to join in and play along.

Original transcription (0:29):

Track 10

Let's start by playing a slow 12/8 blues beat, where the kick drum is played simultaneously with the hi-hats, and the snare is played on beats 4 and 10.

Next, let's play the same beat, but this time, play beats 9, 10, and 12 on the snare drum instead of on the hi-hat.

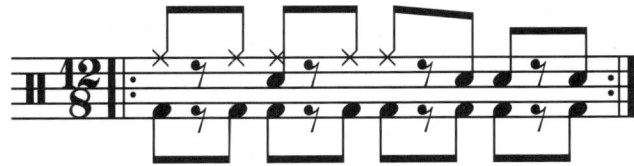

Finally, play the same beat as in the previous lesson but this time, add a snare hit on beat 11, and you'll be playing the blues groove just like Willie Smith plays it on the recording!

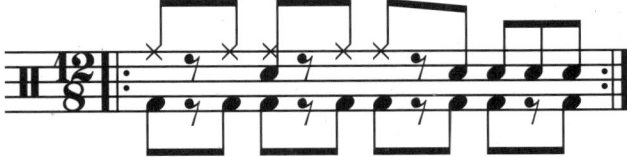

18 BASIC BLUES AND SHUFFLE BEATS

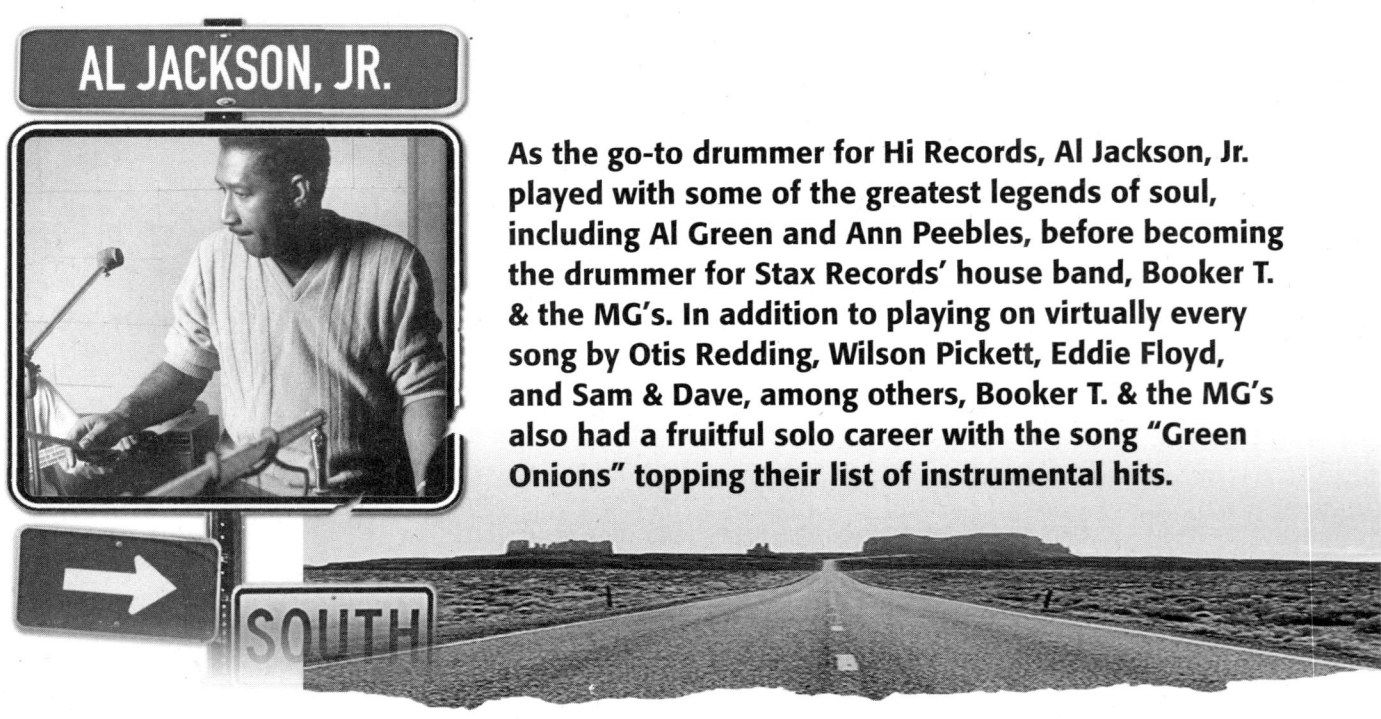

As the go-to drummer for Hi Records, Al Jackson, Jr. played with some of the greatest legends of soul, including Al Green and Ann Peebles, before becoming the drummer for Stax Records' house band, Booker T. & the MG's. In addition to playing on virtually every song by Otis Redding, Wilson Pickett, Eddie Floyd, and Sam & Dave, among others, Booker T. & the MG's also had a fruitful solo career with the song "Green Onions" topping their list of instrumental hits.

"Green Onions"
FROM BOOKER T. & THE MG'S *GREEN ONIONS* (1962)

Al Jackson Jr. was the drummer in the band Booker T. & the MG's, the house band for Stax records, who provided the music foundation for many of the best blues, soul, and R&B acts to come out of Memphis. "Green Onions" is one of the band's most popular hits and is a great tune that demonstrates how a relatively simple-looking beat can actually be quite difficult to master.

Original transcription (0:07):

Track 11

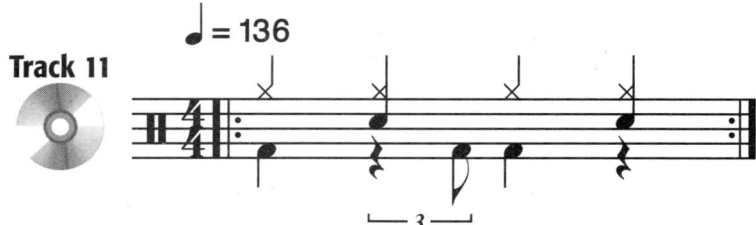

Let's begin by playing quarter notes on the ride cymbal, the kick on beats 1 and 3, and the snare on beats 2 and 4.

Now, add a kick hit on the "let" of beat 2. You may have to practice this slowly at first before increasing the tempo, but, with a little patience, you'll be playing the groove just like Al Jackson Jr.!

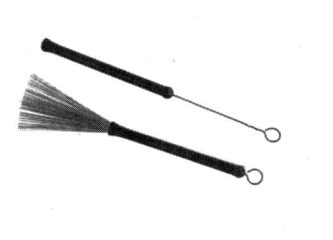

Wire Brushes

Wire brushes are special "sticks" used by drummers to achieve a softer sound. Wire brushes have a wood, plastic, or rubber handle with dozens of thin wires fanning out on the opposite end. Unlike drumsticks, which are made of wood and therefore achieve a loud, defined sound when they strike a cymbal or drumhead, wire brushes achieve a soft, warm sound.

"At Last" (ex. 1)
FROM ETTA JAMES'S *AT LAST* (1961)

Etta James delivers one of the world's greatest blues performances on this track from her debut album. The drummer plays between two basic grooves. In this transcription, we'll focus on the first and simpler of the two grooves. The softer drum sound you hear on the recording is achieved by playing with wire brushes instead of drumsticks.

Original transcription (0:21):

Track 12

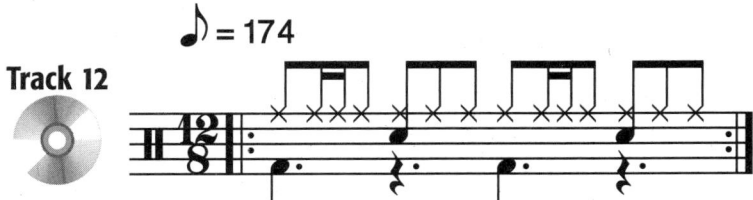

Let's begin by playing a basic 12/8 groove.

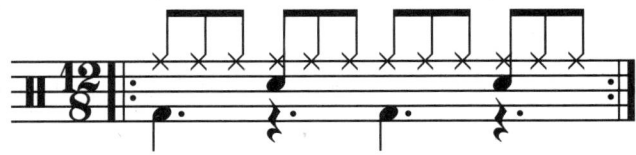

Now, add an extra hi-hat hit evenly spaced between beats 2 and 3 and between beats 8 and 9. You can count this as "1–2–&–3–4–5–6–7–8–&–9–10–11–12." Give it a try!

"At Last" (ex. 2)
FROM ETTA JAMES'S *AT LAST* (1961)

Some sections of this tune demand a bit more intensity in the drum beat. Notice how the drum groove gets a little busier at 0:55.

Original transcription (0:55):

Track 13

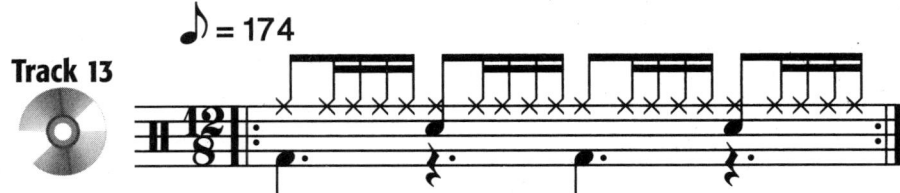

Let's start by playing the first drum groove we learned on the previous transcription.

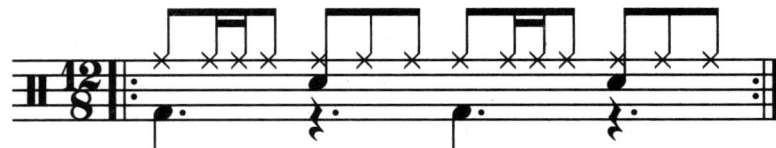

Now, let's add an extra hi-hat hit evenly spaced between beats 3 and 4, and another hi-hat hit between beats 9 and 10.

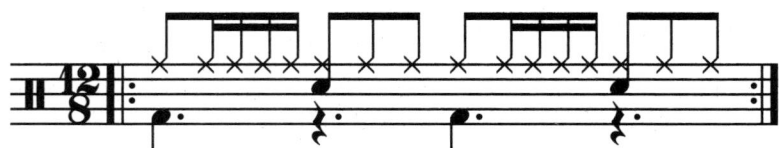

Finally, apply that busy, bouncy hi-hat to these other sections of the groove, and with a little practice, you'll have learned everything you need to know to play along with this classic blues tune.

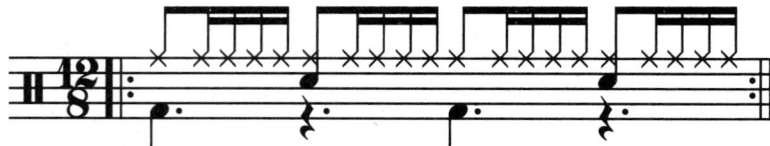

"Texas Flood"
FROM STEVIE RAY VAUGHAN AND DOUBLE TROUBLE'S *TEXAS FLOOD* (1983)

Chris Layton had the divine privilege of playing the drums for one of the greatest blues guitarists of all time—Stevie Ray Vaughan. Layton is a gifted blues drummer with a talent for laying down the perfect drum groove to complement Stevie's brilliant playing. Check out the groove Layton plays in this popular tune from Vaughan's debut album.

Original transcription (0:01):

Track 14

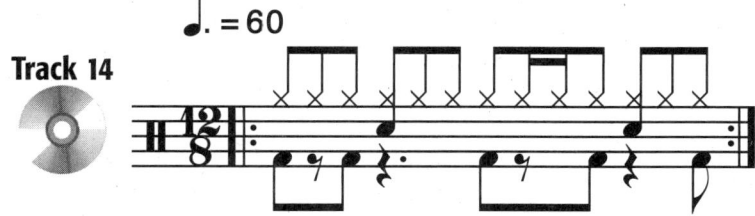

Let's start by playing a simplified 12/8 blues groove with steady eighth notes on the ride cymbal, snare on beats 4 and 10, and kick on beats 1, 3, 7, and 9.

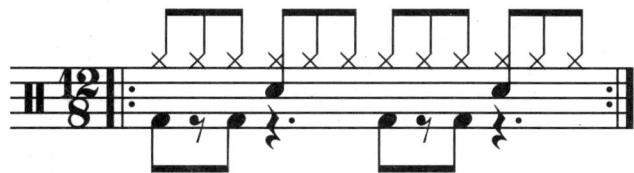

Next, let's add an additional hit on the ride cymbal that's spaced between beats 8 and 9. To play beat 9 and the hit that precedes it quickly enough, you'll need to bounce the stick off the cymbal. Start by hitting the ride cymbal like you normally would with the whipping, or casting, motion, but this time, let the stick bounce off the surface. The next step is to try it again, but this time, after the stick hits the cymbal and bounces once, tighten your fingers and catch the drumstick as you lift it off the surface. This "snap, bounce, catch" motion will help you play faster patterns like this, and will also help you learn to play drum rolls later. Let's try playing this beat with the "snap, bounce, catch" technique. Practice slowly at first and be patient. You can do this!

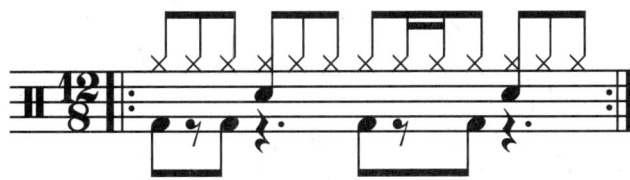

Finally, add one more kick hit on beat 12, and you'll be playing the same drum beat that Chris Layton plays on the song!

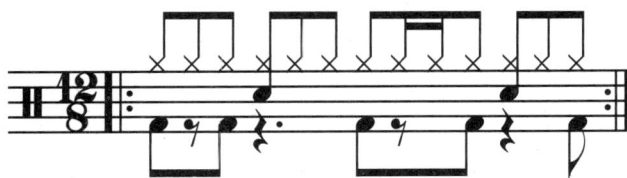

BASIC BLUES AND SHUFFLE BEATS

Chris Layton was the longstanding drummer in Double Trouble, Stevie Ray Vaughan's backing band from 1978 up until Stevie's tragic death in 1990. One of the most decorated drummers in blues history, Layton earned four Grammy awards and played on seven platinum albums with Stevie Ray Vaughan and Double Trouble, including *Blues Explosion, In Step,* and *The Sky Is Crying.*

"Pride and Joy"
FROM STEVIE RAY VAUGHAN AND DOUBLE TROUBLE'S *TEXAS FLOOD* (1983)

Chris Layton plays a commanding shuffle beat that's loaded with some very tasty snare drum work. Notice all the soft ghost note hits on the snare drum that fall between the loud accented backbeats on 2 and 4.

Original transcription (0:07):

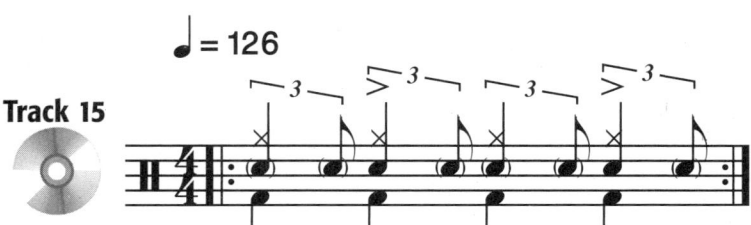

Ghost Notes

A *ghost note* is played softer than the other notes around it.

When notated, a ghost note looks like this:

First, let's break the beat down into its most basic elements by playing quarter notes on the ride and the kick, and the snare on beats 2 and 4.

Next, let's add ghost notes on the snare drum on beats 1 and 3. Try to create a very big difference in volume between the ghost notes on beats 1 and 3 and the accented notes on beats 2 and 4.

BASIC BLUES AND SHUFFLE BEATS 23

Now, let's add some more ghost notes on the snare, this time on the "let" of beats 2 and 4. Practice this at a very slow tempo, and gradually increase the speed as you feel comfortable.

Finally, let's add additional snare ghost notes on the "let" of beats 1 and 3. This is a bit tricky at first and requires you to play a very soft note quickly followed by a very loud note, all with your left hand. Start by playing this groove at a very slow tempo and pay close attention to playing the ghost notes very soft and the accented notes very loud. These dynamics, or contrasts in volume, is what make the beat really groove, so practice this until you can play it comfortably. Playing this beat will also develop strength and dexterity in your left hand, which will help you become a better drummer. So stick with it and you will see positive results!

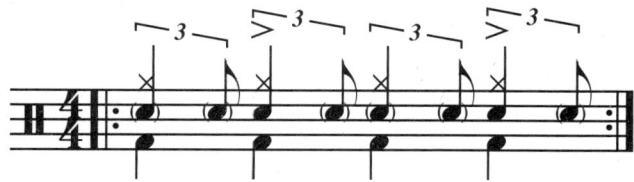

"Move It On Over"
FROM GEORGE THOROGOOD & THE DESTROYERS' *MOVE IT ON OVER* (1978)

You may notice that the drum groove in this tune is very similar to the beat Bonham plays on Led Zeppelin's "You Shook Me," except for one major thing—"Move It On Over" is faster—much, MUCH faster!

Original transcription (0:07):

Track 16

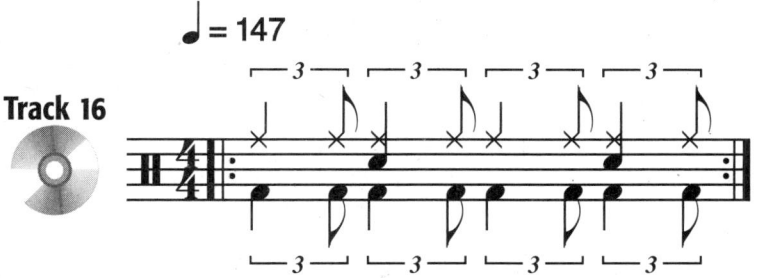

Let's build up our endurance by first focusing on the hi-hat. Start by playing this beat at a comfortable tempo, and gradually increase the speed until you reach the tempo of the song. Practice playing the beat at the marked tempo until you can play it for 60 seconds straight, and remember to relax if you feel your arm starting to tense up.

24 BASIC BLUES AND SHUFFLE BEATS / BASIC BLUES AND SHUFFLE FILLS

Now, let's work on building your endurance by focusing on the kick drum. Again, start by playing this beat at a comfortable tempo and gradually increase the speed until you reach the tempo of the song. Practice playing the beat at the marked tempo until you can play it for 60 seconds straight, and remember to relax if you feel your foot starting to tense up.

Now that we've built up your endurance separately on both the hi-hat and the kick drum, it's time to put both parts together. You may have to start at a slower tempo, but with some practice, you'll be playing this smokin' shuffle beat just like Jeff Simon plays it on the recording!

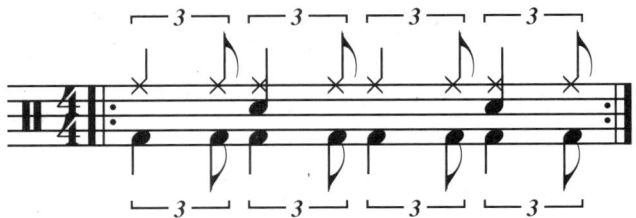

BASIC BLUES AND SHUFFLE FILLS

"You Shook Me"
FROM LED ZEPPELIN'S *LED ZEPPELIN* (1969)

John Bonham plays a simple eighth-note fill on the snare, floor tom, and kick to set up the beat he plays for the remainder of the tune. Let's begin by playing the drum fill and ending it with a simultaneous kick and crash hit on beat 1 of the following measure.

Original transcription (0:04):

Track 17

Now, play the beat after you play the fill, just like Bonham played it on the recording.

Track 18

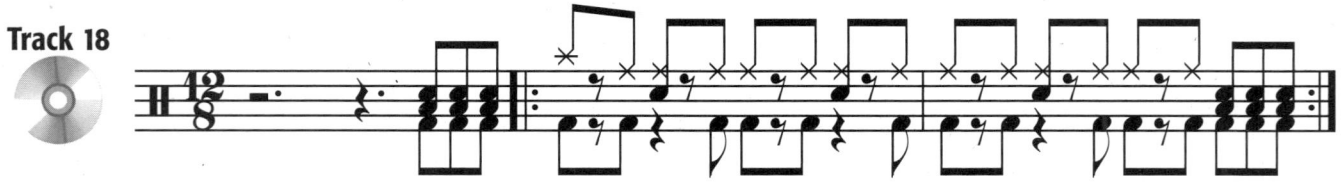

BASIC BLUES AND SHUFFLE FILLS 25

"Bad to the Bone"
FROM GEORGE THOROGOOD & THE DESTROYERS' *BAD TO THE BONE* (1982)

Jeff Simon's fill on the intro of "Bad to the Bone" builds on the same type of fill that Bonham played on "You Shook Me" and adds some embellishments that closely tie in with George Thorogood's catchy guitar riff. Let's try playing the fill by itself, ending with a simultaneous kick and crash hit on beat 1 of the following measure.

Original transcription (0:06):

Track 19

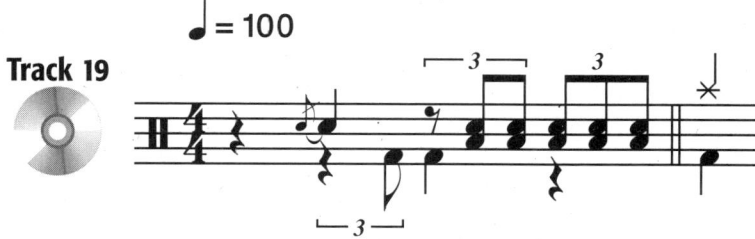

Now, try playing the fill right into the beat of the song, just like it's played on the original recording.

Track 20

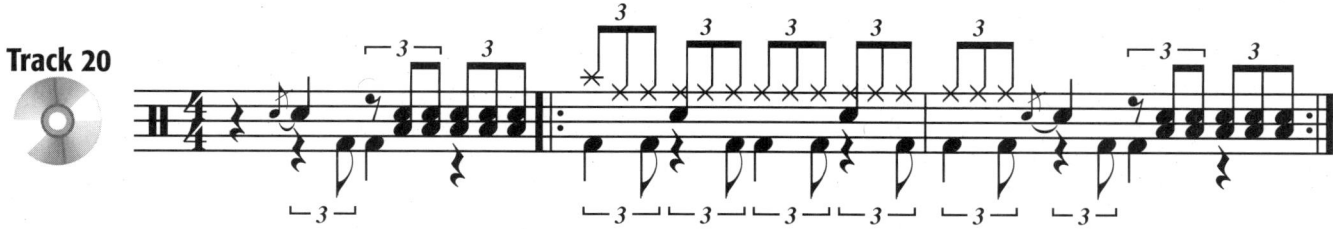

"Texas Flood"
FROM STEVIE RAY VAUGHAN AND DOUBLE TROUBLE'S *TEXAS FLOOD* (1983)

Chris Layton cues the band with this short fill that starts with a drag on the snare on beat 10, carries through with high tom and floor tom hits on beats 11 and 12, respectively, and ends with a simultaneous kick and ride hit on beat 1 of the following measure. Go ahead and try playing the drum fill just like Layton plays it on the recording.

Original transcription (Intro):

Track 21

Now, try playing the drum fill as smoothly as you can, right into the drum beat for the song. Notice that a very similar drum fill occurs at the end of measure 2 of the tune. Practice the fill that leads into the beat, and also the fill leading out of the beat, until you can play them both comfortably and smoothly.

Track 22

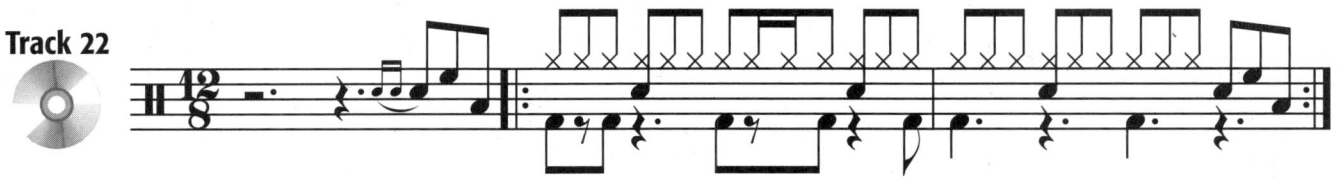

26 BASIC BLUES AND SHUFFLE FILLS

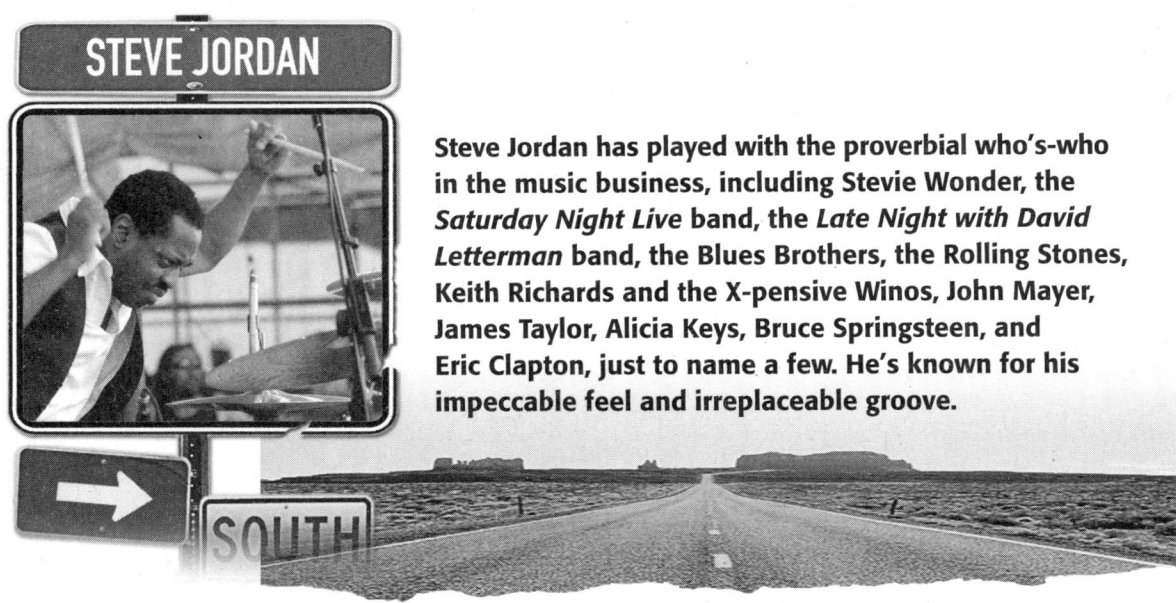

Steve Jordan has played with the proverbial who's-who in the music business, including Stevie Wonder, the *Saturday Night Live* band, the *Late Night with David Letterman* band, the Blues Brothers, the Rolling Stones, Keith Richards and the X-pensive Winos, John Mayer, James Taylor, Alicia Keys, Bruce Springsteen, and Eric Clapton, just to name a few. He's known for his impeccable feel and irreplaceable groove.

"Sweet Home Chicago" (ex. 1)
FROM THE BLUES BROTHERS' *THE BLUES BROTHERS SOUNDTRACK* (1980)

This song is built on a standard 12-bar blues form, which means the band plays sections that are in groups of 12 bars (measures). At the end of the 12th bar, there is something called a *turnaround*. The turnaround is a special fill that concludes the first 12-bar section and sets up the next 12-bar section. This is a very common musical element you will encounter as you listen to the blues. In this example, Steve Jordan plays the following turnaround fill, as notated here. Go ahead and try to play this fill on your own.

Original transcription (0:29):

Track 23

Now, here's how the entire 12-bar section looks when it's notated on paper. Notice that the same fill we just learned is now placed in measure 12 of this 12-bar blues section. Go ahead and play, then repeat, the entire section. It may be helpful to either play along with the song on your headphones or sing to yourself while you play along on the drums.

Track 24

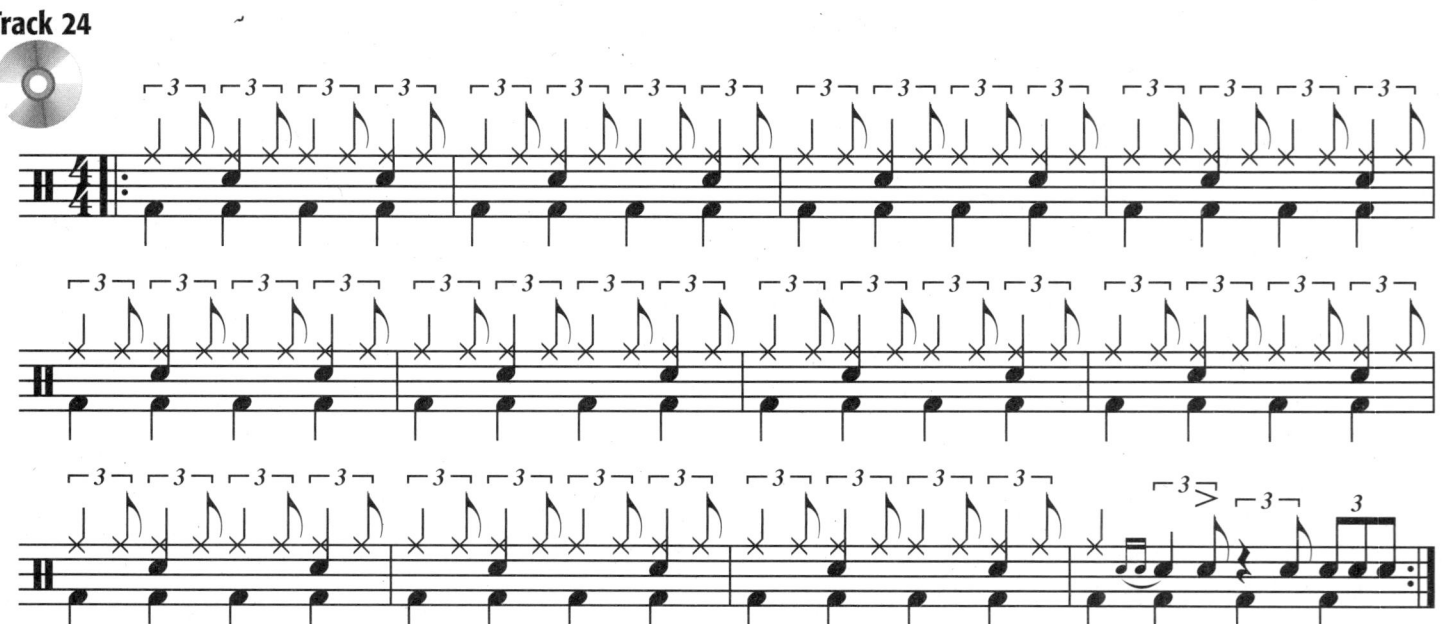

"Sweet Home Chicago" (ex. 2)
FROM THE BLUES BROTHERS' *THE BLUES BROTHERS SOUNDTRACK* (1980)

This tune features a nice big drum fill that sets up and kicks in the solo section of the song. Go ahead and try playing the entire one-bar fill, and end it by simultaneously hitting the kick and crash on beat 1 of the following measure.

Original transcription (3:09):

Track 25

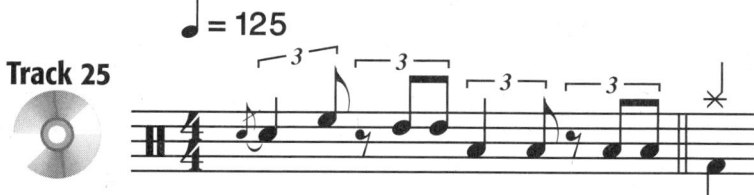

Now, try playing the fill within the context of the beat.

Track 26

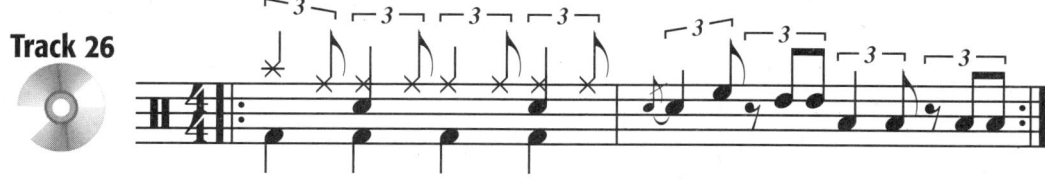

"Stone Crazy"
FROM BUDDY GUY'S *BUDDY'S BLUES* (1997, SINGLE ORIGINALLY RELEASED IN 1962)

Fred Below uses some perfectly placed double-stroke rolls to make this drum fill flow through the music so nicely. Each roll in this example is a *9-stroke roll*, meaning the surface is struck nine times throughout the course of the roll. The first 9-stroke roll starts with the right stick on beat 8 and carries through until the ride is struck with the right stick on beat 10. The actual sticking is RR–LL–RR–LL–R, with all hits played on the snare drum except for the final right hand hit, which is played on the ride cymbal. The second roll mimics the phrasing of the first and starts on beat 11, and carries through until the ride is struck on beat 1 of the following measure. Go ahead and try playing the fill, and pay attention to keeping the rolls nice and even.

The Double-Stroke Roll

Earlier, we learned the "snap, bounce, catch" technique for playing patterns on the ride cymbal. That same technique is used to play drum rolls. To play a double-stroke roll, each stick alternates between this "snap, bounce, catch" motion to create two hits on the drum. Start playing this slowly, using the sticking RR–LL–RR–LL–RR–LL–RR–LL–RR–LL–RR–LL, and so on. Once you get comfortable playing two consecutive hits with each stick and alternating between your left and right hands, begin to speed this exercise up paying close attention to making the notes sound as evenly spaced as possible. When done perfectly, it's hard to tell you are alternating hands or bouncing your sticks, because each drum hit should sound the same. When notated, double-stroke rolls look like this:

Original transcription (0:55):

Track 27

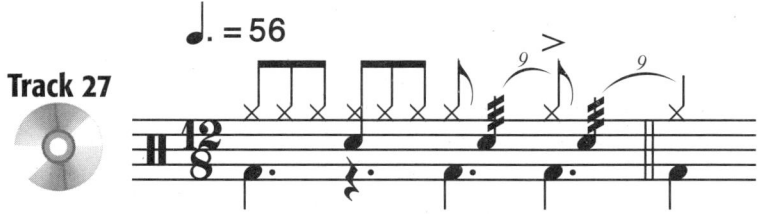

Now try playing the fill in the context of the drum beat. Practice until you can play the entire phrase smoothly and comfortably.

Track 28

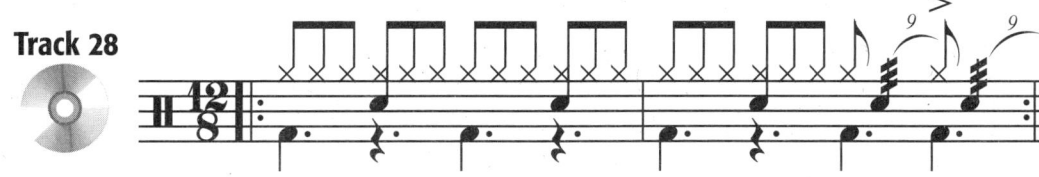

"Pride and Joy"
FROM STEVIE RAY VAUGHAN AND DOUBLE TROUBLE'S *TEXAS FLOOD* (1983)

Chris Layton plays *stop time* on this tune, which is quite common for the genre and found in hundreds of 12-bar blues songs. The stops start in bar 1 and continue to a triplet build on bar 4. This example begins on bar 12 of a 12-bar blues section, continues with the four measures of stop time, and concludes by leading-in to bar 5 of the 12-bar blues section.

Original transcription (1:16):

Let's begin by isolating and playing the short fill that starts on bar 12 of the 12-bar blues section.

Now, let's isolate and repeat the fills that happen on bars 1 and 2 of the stop time section.

Next, let's play bars 3 and 4 of the stop time section and end with a simultaneous kick and ride hit on beat 1 of the following measure.

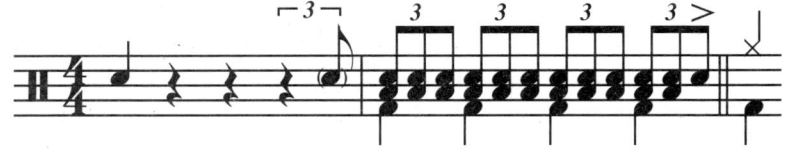

Finally, put all the examples together, and play stop time just like Chris Layton plays it on "Pride and Joy" and thousands of other drummers play it in their blues bands all the time!

"Red House" (ex. 1)
FROM THE JIMI HENDRIX EXPERIENCE'S *ARE YOU EXPERIENCED* (1997 REMASTERED VERSION)

Mitch Mitchell plays a one-bar fill that alternates masterfully between both his hands on the toms and snare, and his foot on the kick drum.

Original transcription (0:13):

Track 30

Let's begin by removing the flams from the fill and playing this pattern that alternates between simultaneous hits on the snare drum and floor tom, and the kick drum played with your foot. Notice that beats 10 and 11 are played consecutively on the snare and floor tom, and beats 12 and 1 of the following measure are played consecutively on the kick with a big crash hit also occurring on beat 1 of the following measure.

Now, let's move the hands around the drums so the fill sounds just like Mitch Mitchell played it on the recording. Your left hand will hit the snare drum on beats 2, 4, 6, and 8, while your right hand moves from the flam played on the snare on beat 2 to the high tom on beat 4, to the floor tom on beat 6, and back to a flam on the snare on beat 8. Beat 10 is played by simultaneously hitting the high tom and floor tom, and beat 11 is played by simultaneously hitting the two floor toms. If you don't have a second floor tom, substitute a rack tom for this hit. The fill concludes with a kick drum hit on beat 12 and a simultaneous kick and crash hit on beat 1 of the following measure. Go ahead and give it a try!

Finally, try playing the fill and then immediately follow it with the drum beat just like Mitch Mitchell played on the recording.

Track 31

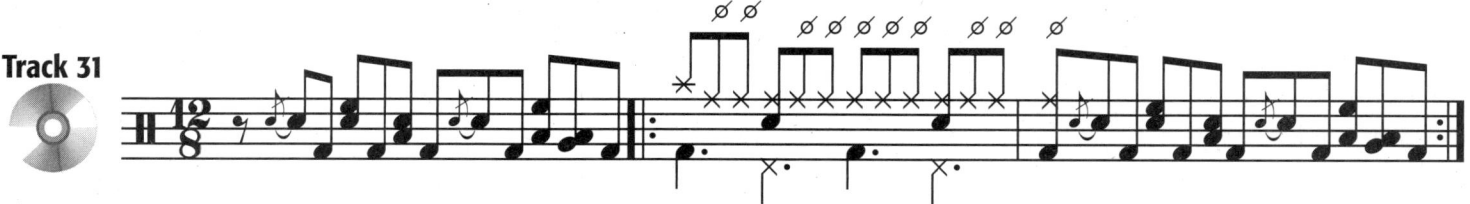

Improvisation

Improvisation means making up the music you're playing as you go along. Instead of playing predetermined beats and fills, improvisation is a totally spontaneous type of music where you can play anything that comes to your mind.

The Fermata

A *fermata* is used to indicate that a note should be sustained longer than its note value. A fermata is typically used at the end of a piece of music, and the musician holds the note as long as necessary. The length of a fermata is subjective and usually determined by the musician, or the conductor, depending on the musical setting. A fermata looks like this:

"Red House" (ex. 2)
FROM THE JIMI HENDRIX EXPERIENCE'S *ARE YOU EXPERIENCED* (1997 REMASTERED VERSION)

This tune features a great drum fill that helps the entire band end the song. This is a fairly typical ending you'll hear in many blues tunes, so once you learn to play it here, you'll be able to apply it, and similar fills, to the end of a wide variety of blues songs. Go ahead and try playing the complete fill as notated below. After you hit the simultaneous kick and crash hits on beats 4 and 7 of the third measure below, go crazy and play any kind of fill you want until you're ready to hit the final note and end the song. This is a place where you can improvise. Give it a try, and have fun with it!

Original transcription (3:32):

Track 32

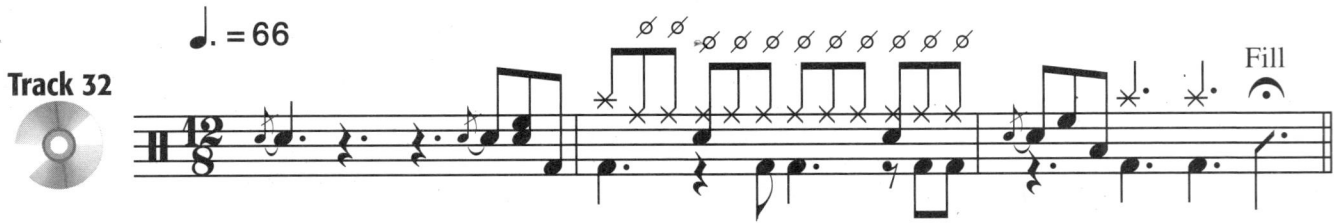

IRV COTTLER

Among the most respected drummers of the big band era, Irv Cottler recorded with Louis Armstrong, Bing Crosby, Sammy Davis, Jr., Dean Martin, Mel Tormé, and Ella Fitzgerald, among others, but it was with Frank Sinatra that Cottler made his biggest mark. Cottler played with Sinatra for over 30 years, and together they released some of the most beloved songs in history.

BASIC JAZZ BEATS

"Everybody Loves Somebody"
FROM DEAN MARTIN'S *DREAM WITH DEAN* (1964)

Drummer Irv Cottler plays a simple jazz groove on this famous song made popular by Dean Martin in 1964. This basic triplet groove is played in 4/4 time at a moderate tempo. It's played very similarly to some of the blues grooves learned earlier in this book, so, for the most part, this should be a review of what you already know, only set to jazz instead of blues.

Original transcription (0:11):

Track 33

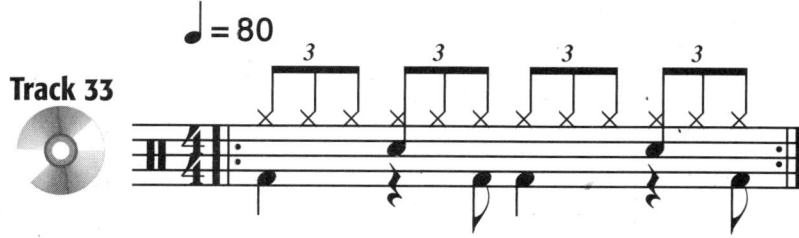

The Rim Click

The *rim click* is a technique where the tip of the stick is placed on the drumhead near one side of the rim while the butt end of the stick is struck down against the rim on the opposite side. The resulting sound is a sharp high-pitched click.

When notated, a rim click looks like this:

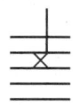

"What a Wonderful World"
FROM LOUIE ARMSTRONG'S *ALL TIME GREATEST HITS* (SONG ORIGINALLY RECORDED IN 1968)

Grady Tate's drum beat in this famous Louie Armstrong song is similar to the beat we just played on "Everybody Loves Somebody," except in "What a Wonderful World," the tempo is slower, the middle beat of each triplet on the ride cymbal is removed, and a rim click is played on beats 2 and 4.

Original transcription (Intro):

Track 34

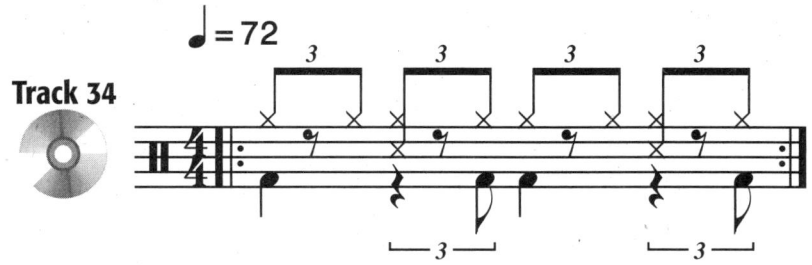

"I've Got You Under My Skin"
FROM MICHAEL BUBLÉ'S *IT'S TIME* (2005)

Drummer Jeff Hamilton demonstrates a classic and incredibly versatile swing beat in Michael Bublé's rendition of the Cole Porter original "I've Got You Under My Skin." In this classic beat, the kick drum is played softly on beats 1, 2, 3, and 4; the hi-hat is played with the left foot on beats 2 and 4; a rim click is played on beats 2 and 4; and the ride cymbal is played on beats 1, 2, 3, and 4, and on the "&" of beats 2 and 4. This is a very important drum beat to master because it will work well in most jazz tunes. Start slowly, and gradually increase the tempo as you feel comfortable.

Original transcription (1:12):

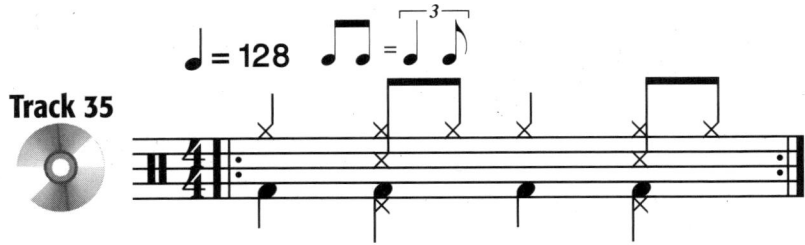

Track 35

Although the ride cymbal is notated with eighth notes, it's meant to be swung, that is, the groove is intended to be played with a bouncy "swinging" feel instead of a "straight" rock feel. This is usually indicated by inserting the word "swung" at the beginning of the drum notation, or by adding a small notation like this:

It's very common to see jazz songs notated this way, especially when tempos are above 100 bpm, because it's easier to read and write. All the following notations describe the same basic jazz ride cymbal pattern, but we'll focus on the notation style "D" in this book for swing beats over 100 bpm.

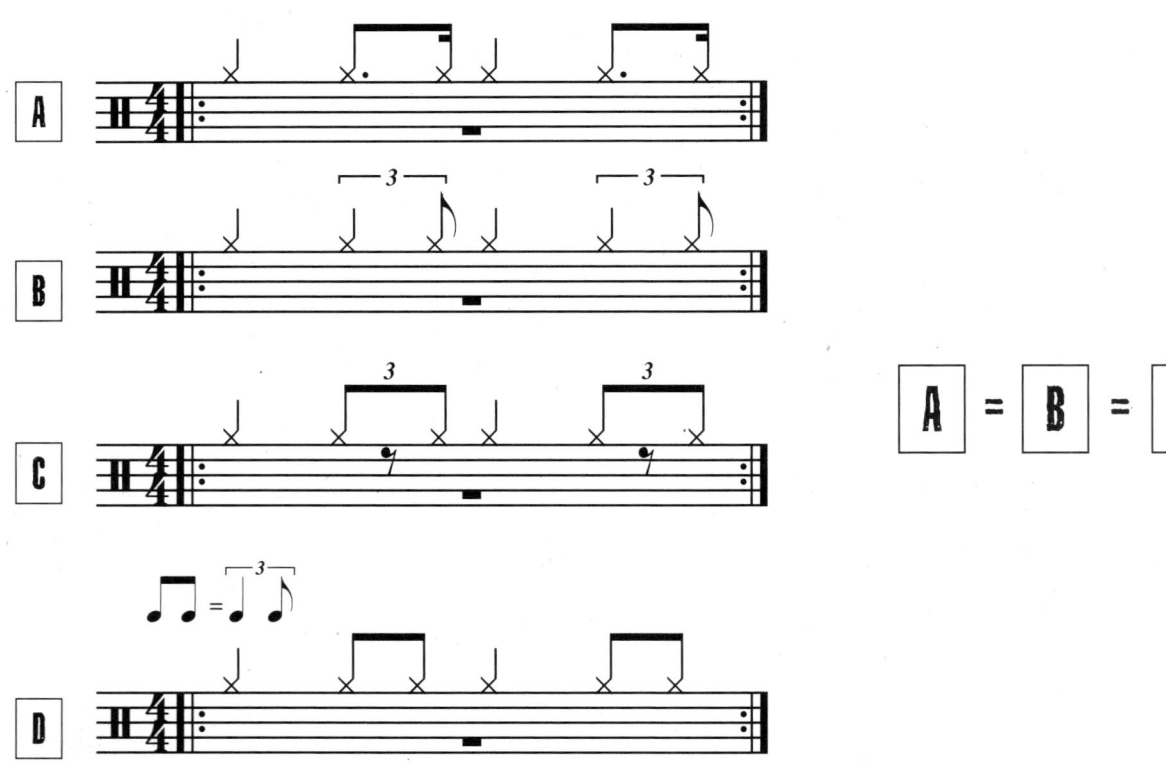

"Theme from New York, New York"
FROM FRANK SINATRA'S *TRILOGY: PAST PRESENT AND FUTURE* (1980)

Irv Cottler takes the basic swing beat learned in the previous lesson and modifies it to more closely fit the "vibe" of what the other instruments are playing on this iconic tune. Cottler plays the hi-hat (slightly open) instead of the ride cymbal, the kick on beats 1 and 3, the snare on beats 2 and 4, and the crash cymbal on beat 2. Go ahead and give it a try!

Original transcription (0:01):

Track 36

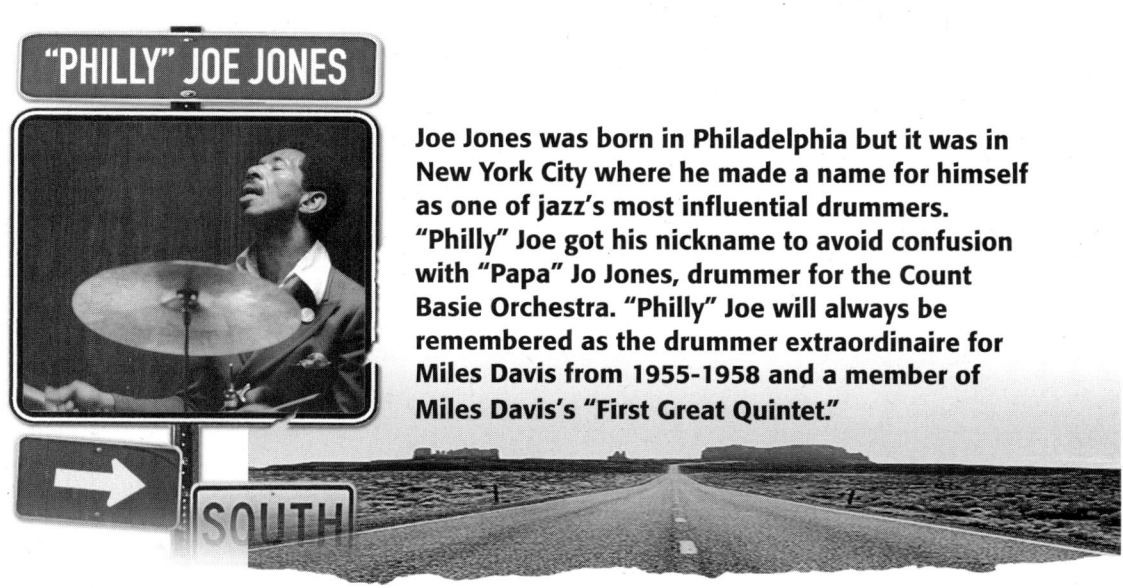

Joe Jones was born in Philadelphia but it was in New York City where he made a name for himself as one of jazz's most influential drummers. "Philly" Joe got his nickname to avoid confusion with "Papa" Jo Jones, drummer for the Count Basie Orchestra. "Philly" Joe will always be remembered as the drummer extraordinaire for Miles Davis from 1955-1958 and a member of Miles Davis's "First Great Quintet."

"Straight, No Chaser"
FROM MILES DAVIS'S *MILESTONES* (1958)

Miles Davis's "go-to" drummer, "Philly" Joe Jones, plays another adaptation of the standard swing beat in this rendition of the jazz standard composed by Thelonious Monk. The drum beat in this excerpt, played under Red Garland's gorgeous piano solo, features a typical swing pattern on the ride cymbal, a rim click on beat 4, and the hi-hat that's played with the left foot on beats 2 and 4. This tune is played at a brisk tempo that may be too challenging at first, so don't try to play it at this tempo right away. Be sure to practice slowly, and gradually increase the tempo over time as you feel comfortable. Eventually, with some practice, you'll be able to play the beat at this tempo.

Original transcription (6:10):

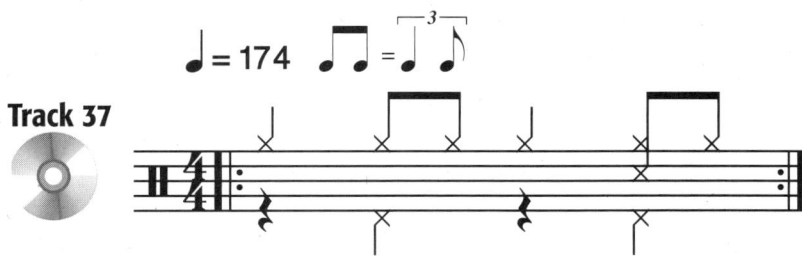

Track 37

"In a Mellow Tone"
FROM DUKE ELLINGTON'S *BEST OF DUKE ELLINGTON* (SONG ORIGINALLY RECORDED IN 1939)

Sonny Greer, drummer on Duke Ellington's earliest recordings, plays a very versatile and useful jazz beat on this popular jazz standard. Greer plays a rim click on beats 2 and 4 and a standard swing beat on the hi-hat, but what makes this beat so interesting is that the hi-hat is opened on beats 1 and 3 and closed on beats 2 and 4. This adds an interesting sonic texture to the swing beat. Go ahead and give it a try! Start slowly at first, and gradually increase the tempo as you feel comfortable.

Original transcription (0:12):

Track 38

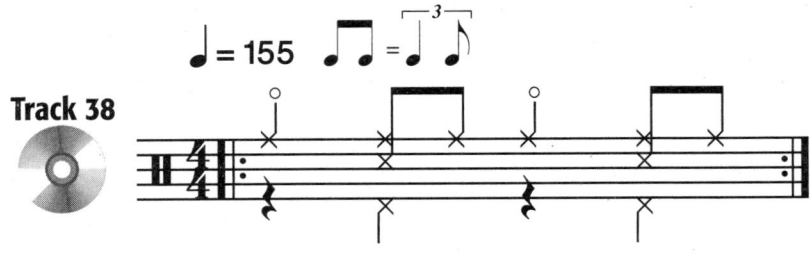

"In the Mood"
FROM THE GLENN MILLER ORCHESTRA'S *BEST OF GLENN MILLER* (SONG ORIGINALLY RECORDED IN 1939)

Drummer Ray McKinley plays a similar beat on "In the Mood" to the beat we just learned from "In a Mellow Tone." In this tune, the open/closed hi-hat swing pattern remains the same, but the kick is played softly on beats 1, 2, 3, and 4, and there are no rim clicks. Go ahead and try playing the beat slowly, and then gradually increase the tempo until you can play it up to speed.

Original transcription (0:12):

Track 39

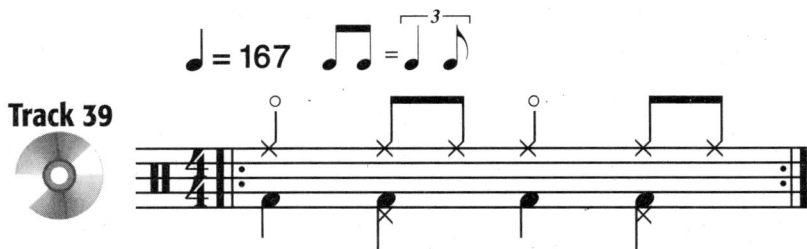

BASIC JAZZ BEATS

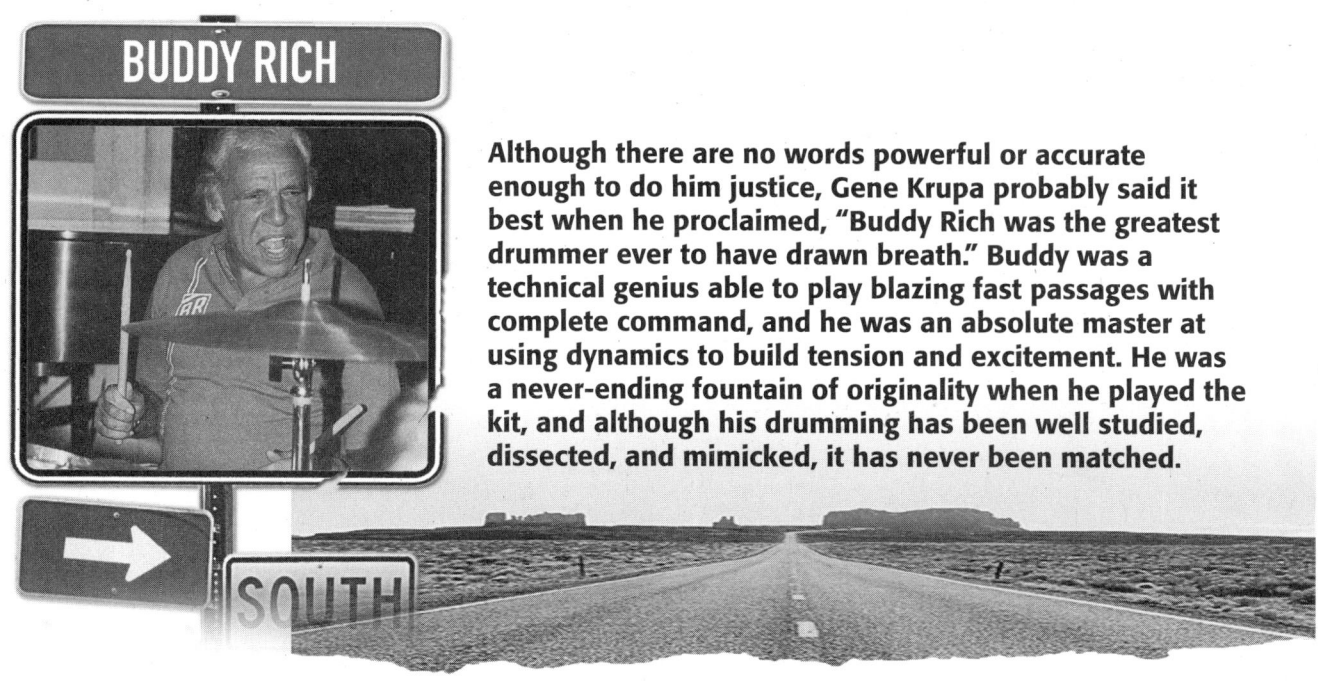

BUDDY RICH

Although there are no words powerful or accurate enough to do him justice, Gene Krupa probably said it best when he proclaimed, "Buddy Rich was the greatest drummer ever to have drawn breath." Buddy was a technical genius able to play blazing fast passages with complete command, and he was an absolute master at using dynamics to build tension and excitement. He was a never-ending fountain of originality when he played the kit, and although his drumming has been well studied, dissected, and mimicked, it has never been matched.

"Chelsea Bridge"
FROM BUDDY RICH'S *THE BEST OF BUDDY RICH (PACIFIC JAZZ)* (1997, SONG ORIGINALLY RECORDED IN 1970)

Buddy Rich is praised by drummers around the world because of his amazing control, speed, and musicality. Buddy didn't always play blazing fast notes whenever he sat behind the drum kit; he knew when to play fast and hard, and when to play slow and soft. This excerpt shows off Buddy's slower, softer musical side.

Original transcription (Intro):

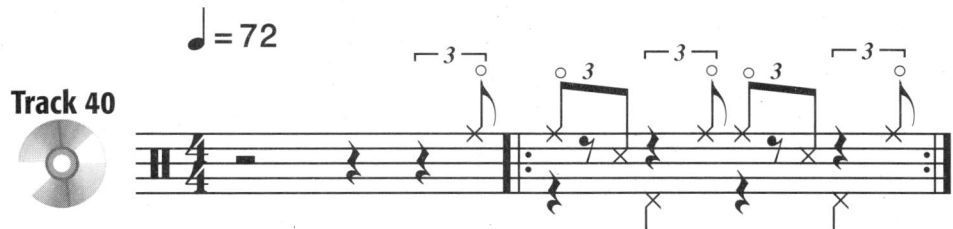

Track 40

Let's start by playing the open hi-hat with your right stick on beats 1 and 3, and on the third note of each triplet on beats 2 and 4, while closing the hi-hat on beats 2 and 4 with your left foot.

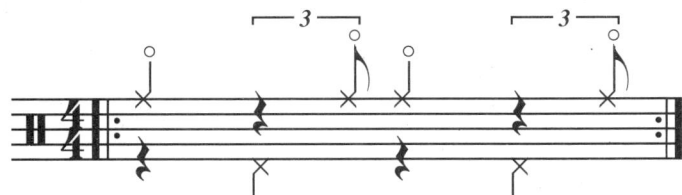

Now, let's play the same beat as in the previous lesson, but this time, let's add a rim click on the third note of each triplet on beats 1 and 3. With a little practice, you'll be playing the groove just like Buddy Rich!

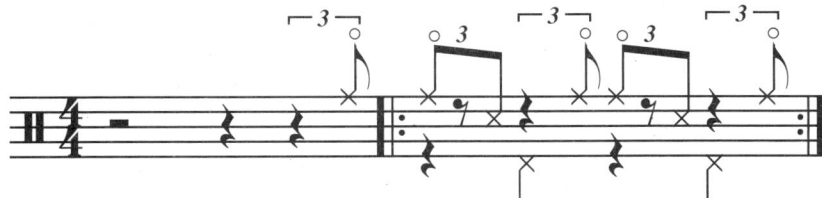

"Blues Walk"
FROM LOU DONALDSON'S *BLUES WALK* (1958)

The excerpt in this lesson is an adaptation that combines the drumset part, played by Dave Bailey, and the conga part, played by Ray Barretto, into a beat that a single drummer can play on the drumset. The standard swing pattern is played with the right hand on the ride cymbal, the hi-hat is played with the left foot on beats 2 and 4, the rim click is played on the snare on beat 2, and the high tom is played with the left hand on beat 4 and on the "&" of beat 4. It will take a little practice to switch back and forth between playing the rim click and regular hits on the drum, so start slowly, and stick with it!

Original transcription (0:01):

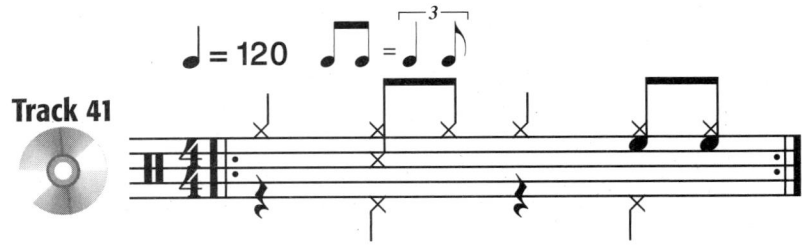

Track 41

Syncopation

Syncopation refers to unexpected rhythms that occur within a groove. Drummers often play lots of syncopated beats in jazz and funk tunes. Jazz drummers often add syncopated hits with their left hand on the snare drum while they "keep time" with a basic swing pattern on the ride cymbal. These syncopated snare hits often vary constantly throughout the song.

"The Sidewinder"
FROM LEE MORGAN'S *THE SIDEWINDER* (1964)

Drummer Billy Higgins plays a catchy swing beat on this tune. Notice how the snare pattern perfectly complements what the piano player is doing. This syncopated drum beat takes coordination, and coordination takes practice, so start by playing each lesson very slowly, and increase the tempo as you feel comfortable.

Original transcription (0:01):

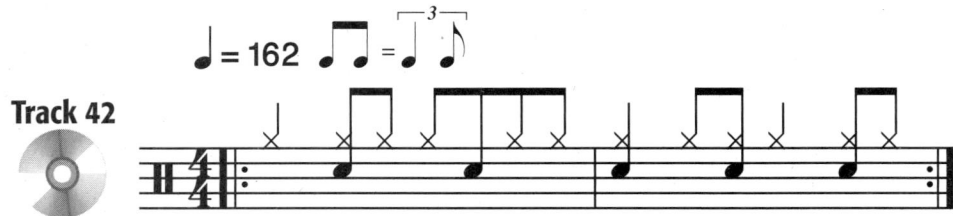

Track 42

Let's start by playing a basic swing pattern on the ride cymbal, and playing the snare on beat 2 of the first measure and on beat 4 of the second measure.

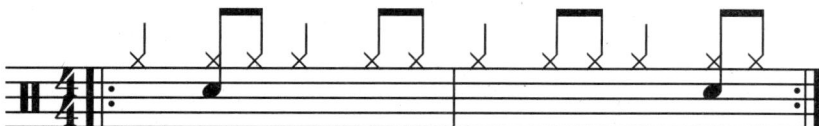

Now, let's play the same beat, but this time, add a snare hit on beat 1 of the second measure.

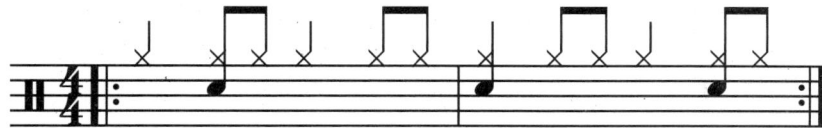

Next, play the same beat, but this time, add another snare hit on the "&" of beat 2 in the second measure.

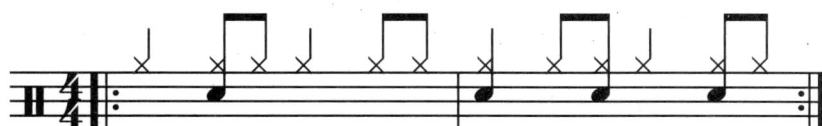

Finally, add one more snare hit, this time on the "&" of beat 3 in the first measure, and you'll be playing the jazz groove just like Billy Higgins plays it on the recording!

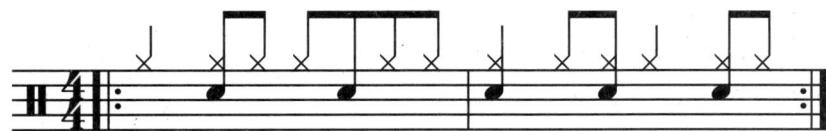

BASIC JAZZ BEATS

Among the first to play both bebop and hard bop jazz styles, Art Blakey was one of the most influential drummers in jazz. He led The Jazz Messengers, one of the longest-running jazz groups in history, which throughout their 30 years showcased a long line of legends including Horace Silver, Clifford Brown, Wayne Shorter, and Freddie Hubbard, to name a few.

"Moanin'"
FROM ART BLAKEY & THE JAZZ MESSENGERS' *MOANIN'* (1958)

Art Blakey led the highly influential Jazz Messengers for over 30 years. This tune features some beautiful playing by Blakey. Notice how he punctuates the music by sometimes adding soft ghosted snare hits right before the backbeat. This is the touch of a master drummer and a skill that's definitely worth learning.

Original transcription (0:30):

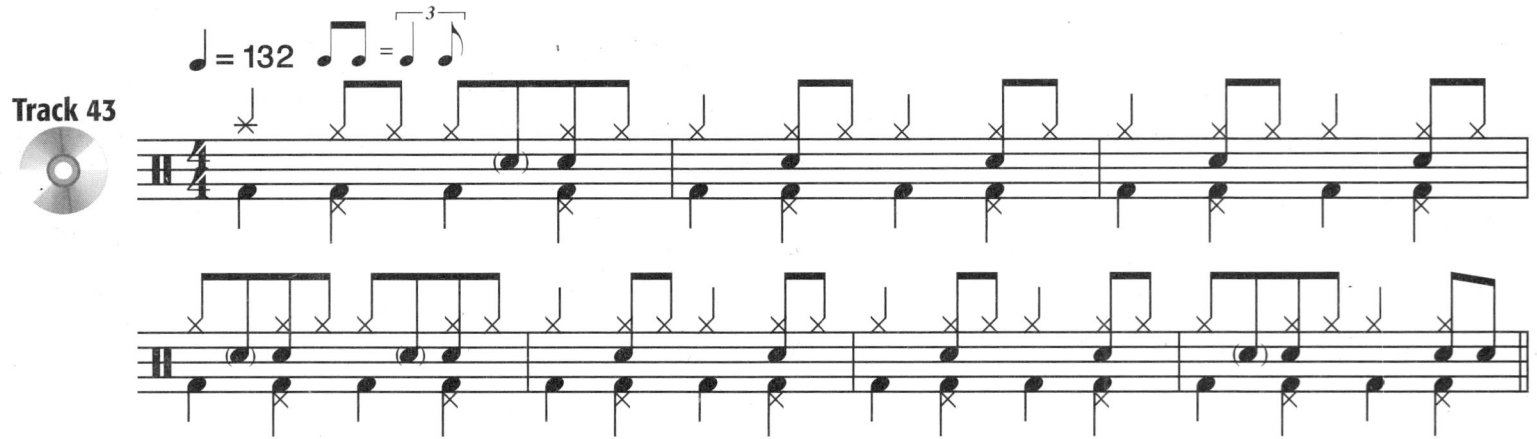

Let's start by playing a basic swing groove with the right hand on the ride, the snare on beats 2 and 4, the kick drum softly on beats 1, 2, 3, and 4 with the right foot, and the hi-hat on beats 2 and 4 with the left foot.

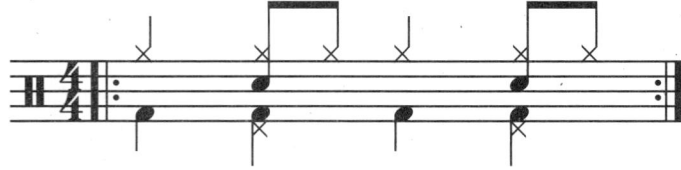

BASIC JAZZ BEATS 39

Next, let's play the same beat, but this time, also play a very soft ghost note on the "&" of beat 3. It will take some practice to play a soft ghosted note on the snare immediately followed by a louder hit on the drum, but stick with it. Practice slowly at first, and gradually increase the tempo as you feel comfortable.

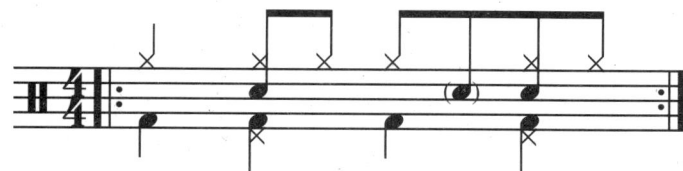

Now, let's play the same beat as in the previous lesson, but add another ghosted snare hit on the "&" of beat 1.

Finally, play the full seven-bar excerpt, which has the ghosted snare hits tastefully placed throughout.

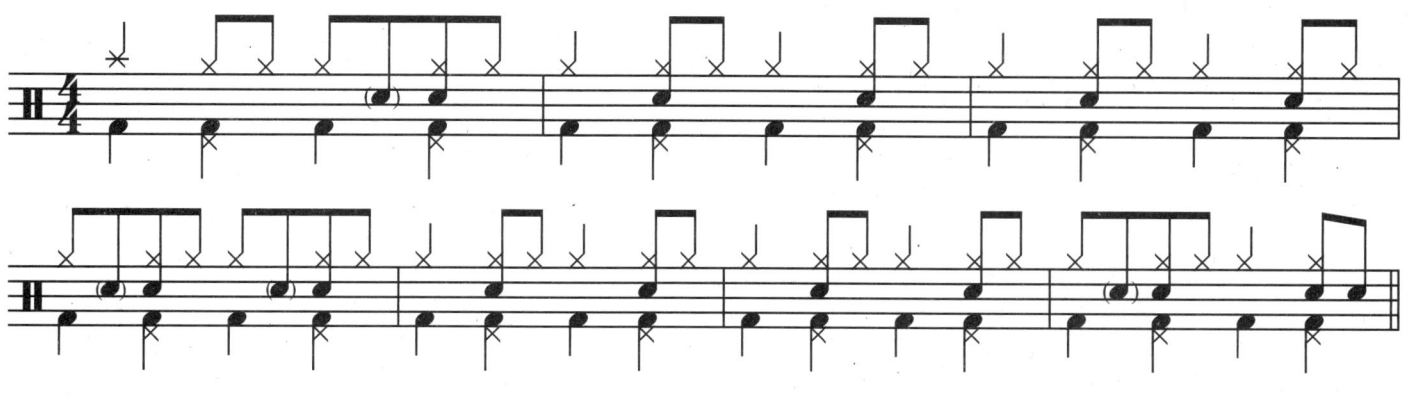

"So What"
FROM MILES DAVIS'S *KIND OF BLUE* (1959)

Many jazz drummers embellish the basic swing beat by adding hits that "color" and "texture" the groove. Drummer Jimmy Cobb plays the standard swing beat with a brush in his right hand on the ride cymbal and the hi-hat with his left foot on beats 2 and 4, and he embellishes the groove by playing the kick drum on beat 3 and on the "&" of beat 4—right in tandem with Miles's trumpet. Go ahead and play the beat just like Jimmy Cobb plays on the recording!

Original transcription (0:52):

Track 44

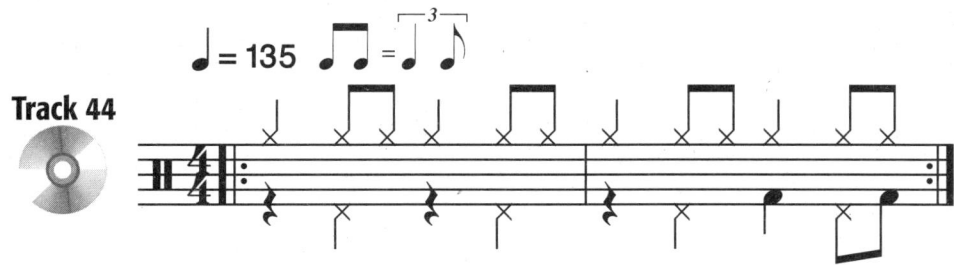

40 BASIC JAZZ BEATS

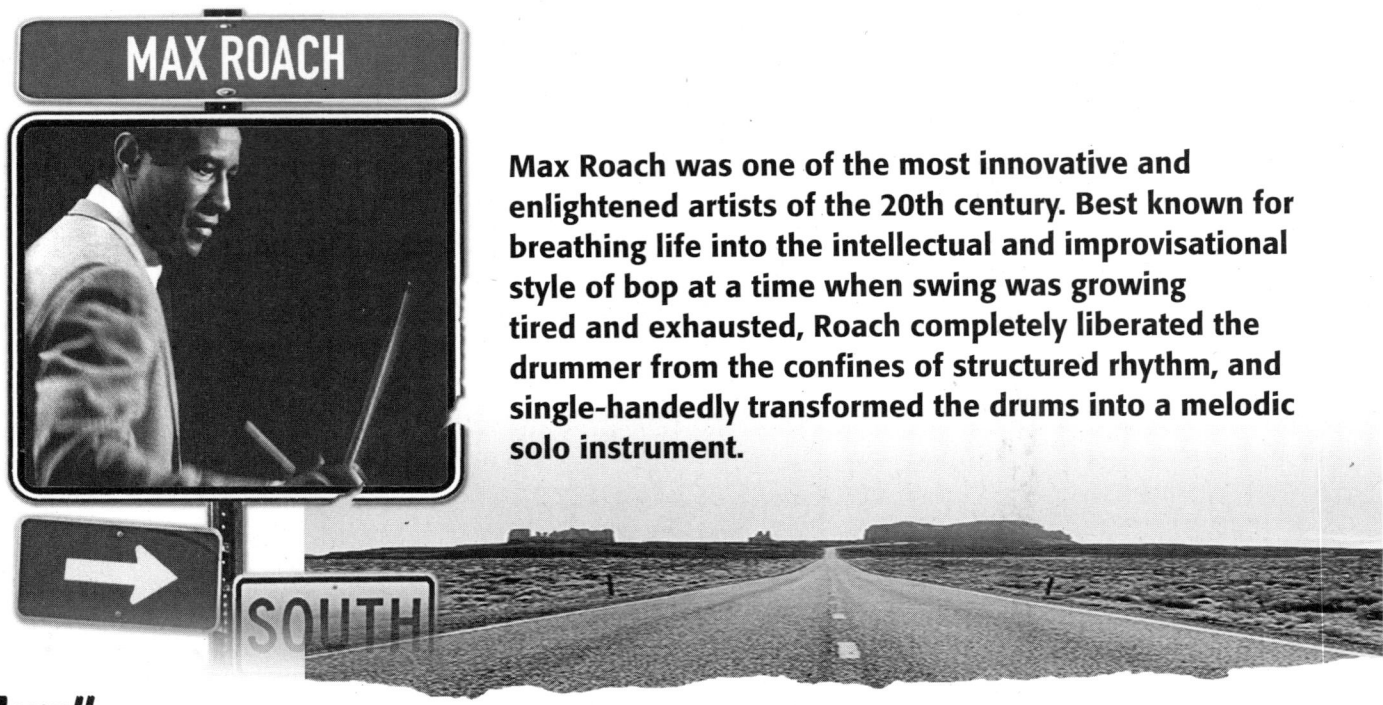

"Jeru"
FROM MILES DAVIS'S *BIRTH OF THE COOL* (1949)

Max Roach was one of the most creative and musically tasteful jazz drummers of all time. On this tune, Max hits all the stops on the snare and kick in perfect sync with the band while adding some very tasteful swing beats on the ride cymbal throughout.

Original transcription (1:30):

Let's start by isolating and repeating the second measure of the excerpt. This exercise demonstrates that a swing beat doesn't always have to be "ding–ding–da-ding–ding–da-ding." You can play all sorts of variations on that basic swing pattern, like the one written here. Give it a try. Start slowly at first, and gradually increase the tempo as you feel comfortable.

Now, let's isolate and repeat the third measure of the excerpt. This demonstrates another variation on the basic swing pattern we've learned.

Next, let's focus on the fourth measure of the excerpt. This example adds the basic swing pattern as well as the three hits that are played simultaneously on the kick and snare. Playing the exercise with the basic swing pattern will help you see where the kick and snare hits are supposed to be played.
Go ahead and give it a try.

Now, let's play the previous beat, but this time, we'll remove the ride cymbal. Notice that the snare and kick hits are played in the exact same places as in the previous lesson.

Finally, let's put it all together and play the excerpt just like the legendary Max Roach plays it on the recording.

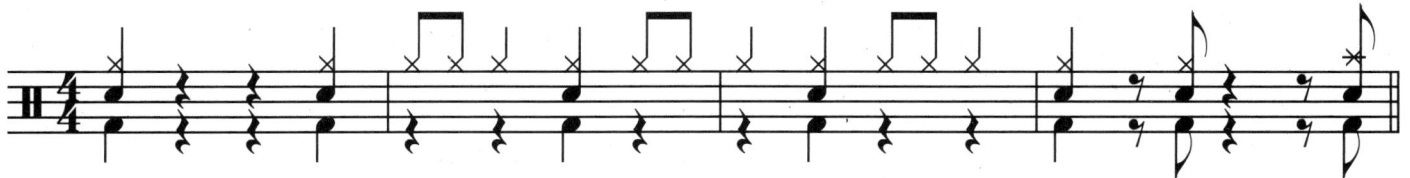

BASIC JAZZ FILLS

"In Walked Bud"
FROM THELONIOUS MONK'S *THE VERY BEST* (2005, SONG ORIGINALLY RELEASED IN 1947)

This fill, played on this tune by Art Blakey, is one of the simplest and most common drum fills you'll find in jazz music. It's incredibly versatile and useful at any tempo, and once you learn this fill, you'll be playing it in jazz songs for the rest of your life. Go ahead and give it a try.

Original transcription (0:24):

Track 46

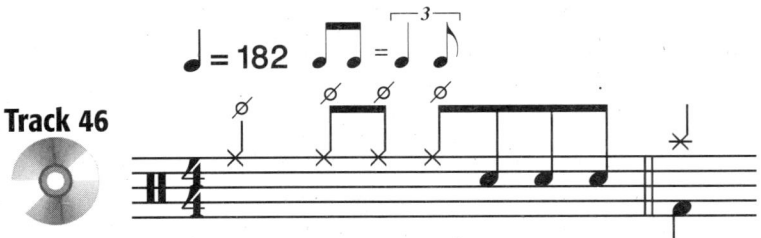

Let's place the fill at the end of a four-bar phrase and practice repeating blocks of four bars of "time" that the fill connects together. Playing time can be any jazz beat you'd like; you choose the swing beat you want to play, and the tempo. The point of this exercise is to show that you can use this simple fill to connect any two passages of jazz music rather effortlessly, even in a swing beat you just made up!

You'll see in this example that there are three bars with four slashes in each. This is music notation shorthand used to indicate playing time. When you see this, play any groove you'd like that's appropriate to the time feel.

Track 47

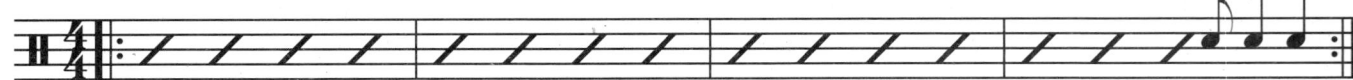

"I've Got You Under My Skin" (ex. 1)
FROM MICHAEL BUBLÉ'S *IT'S TIME* (2005)

This is a second "universal" drum fill that works in nearly any jazz fill application. It's very similar to the previous drum fill, but Jeff Hamilton plays a drag on beat 4 instead of a snare hit on the "&" of beat 3. Go ahead and try playing this versatile drum fill.

Original transcription (1:59):

Track 48

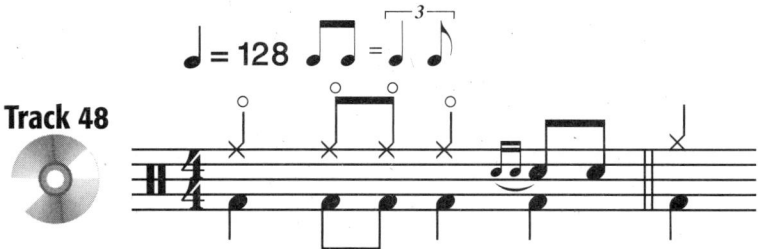

Now, like in the previous lesson, let's improvise a swing beat—anything you'd like to play, and at any tempo you wish—and connect four-bar phrases with this simple drum fill.

Track 49

BASIC JAZZ FILLS   43

Praised for his originality, creativity, sensitivity, dynamics, feel, and musical maturity, Jeff Hamilton is as in-demand as jazz drummers get. Jeff has played the drums on nearly 200 recordings from artists including Natalie Cole, Diana Krall, Oscar Peterson, Barney Kessel, and Ray Brown, to name a few.

"I've Got You Under My Skin" (ex. 2)
FROM MICHAEL BUBLÉ'S *IT'S TIME* (2005)

In this fill, Jeff Hamilton plays strategically placed snare hits to accent the phrase in the horn section. This is a very useful concept drummers employ to give a song more excitement and add pronunciation to certain key phrases.

Original transcription (1:24):

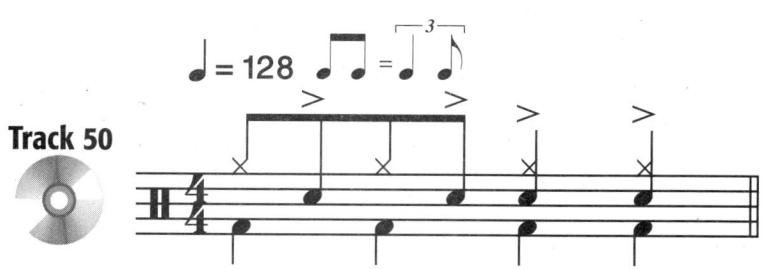

Track 50

Cues

Cues are small notes used in drum charts to communicate a melodic line that is played by another instrument, or several instruments, in the band. The drummer can insert a short fill to set up the band to play the melodic line, or the drummer can play the rhythm along with the other instrument(s) to give the melodic phrase even more impact.

Sometimes you'll see the types of phrases described above written as a cue on a drum chart, like in this example.

Track 51

"I've Got You Under My Skin" (ex. 3)
FROM MICHAEL BUBLÉ'S *IT'S TIME* (2005)

So far, all the drum fills we've explored are played on the snare drum. Fills can also be played all around the drumset. In this excerpt, Jeff Hamilton incorporates the snare, rack tom, kick drum, and hi-hat into his drum fill. Go ahead and give it a try. Start slowly at first, and gradually increase the tempo as you feel comfortable.

Original transcription (1:51):

Track 52

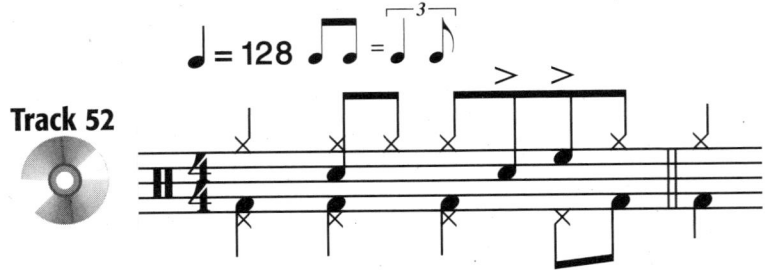

Now, let's practice playing this fill within the context of the beat. In this exercise, we'll play the fill at the end of a repeating four-bar phrase.

Track 53

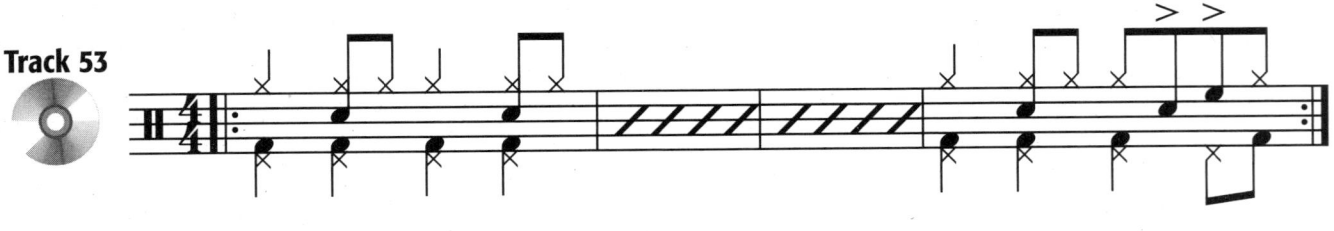

"Theme from New York, New York"
FROM FRANK SINATRA'S *TRILOGY: PAST PRESENT AND FUTURE* (1980)

Irv Cottler plays a dramatic, yet simple, triplet pattern fill on the snare and floor tom to increase the intensity in this section of the song. In this example, the snare and floor tom are played in unison, with the snare played with the left hand and the floor tom played with the right hand.

Original transcription (1:50):

Track 54

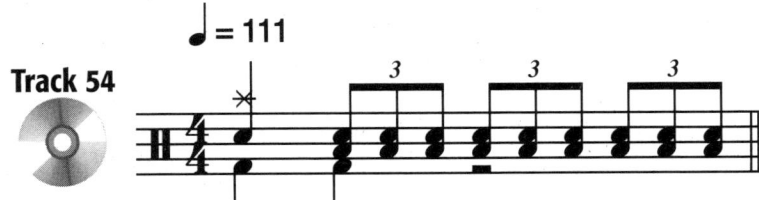

This is a very common fill, especially on jazz tunes played at slow to moderate tempos. Here's an alternative way of playing the fill that adds even more intensity by playing the kick drum on all four beats.

Track 55

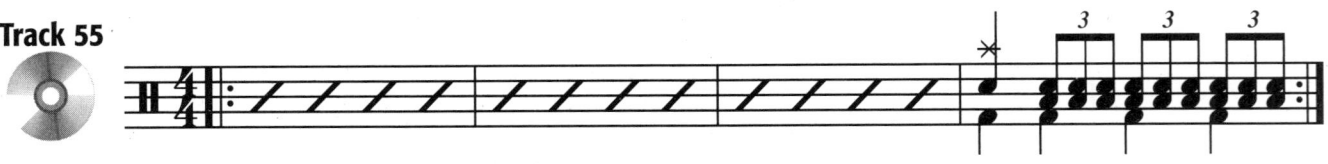

BASIC JAZZ FILLS

The Multiple Bounce Roll (Press Roll, Buzz Roll)

The *multiple bounce roll*, sometimes called a *press roll* or a *buzz roll*, is one of the 40 international drum rudiments. It's played by pressing the sticks into the head in an alternating pattern to create the audible effect of a buzzing, white noise, type of sound. When notated, multiple bounce rolls look like this:

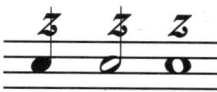

Crescendo and Decrescendo

Crescendo indicates that the volume is gradually increasing. *Decrescendo* indicates that the volume is gradually decreasing. When notated, a crescendo looks like this:

———————

and a decrescendo looks like this:

———————

"Moanin'"
FROM ART BLAKEY & THE JAZZ MESSENGERS' *MOANIN'* (1958)

The multiple bounce roll is another key tool in the jazz drummer's arsenal that can be used as a drum fill to bridge two sections of a song. Art Blakey starts the roll softly in the beginning and gradually crescendos throughout the measure until he hits the crash and kick on beat 1 of the following measure.

Original transcription (0:58):

Track 56

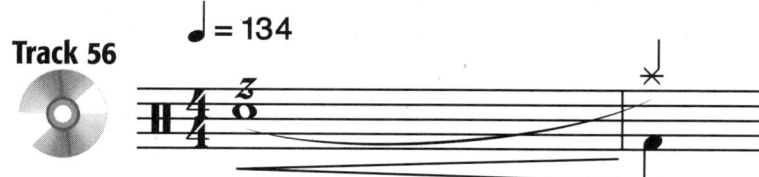

You could also play the press roll with a decrescendo. Let's practice playing with dynamics on this four-bar phrase.

Track 57

Now, let's try it with the dynamic markings reversed. In this exercise, the press roll is played with a crescendo, and the swing beat is played with a decrescendo. Go ahead and give it a try.

Track 58

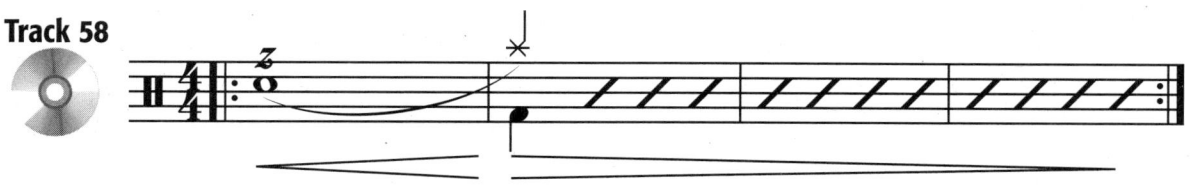

46 BASIC JAZZ FILLS

"In Walked Bud"
FROM THELONIOUS MONK'S *THE VERY BEST* (2005, SONG ORIGINALLY RELEASED IN 1947)

Art Blakey plays a great one-bar drum fill that starts on the snare and finishes on the kick. Notice how Blakey's use of straight (not swung) eighth notes and a sixteenth-note figure really stands out and punctuates the music. Go ahead and give it a try.

Original transcription (2:07):

Track 59

Now, let's practice playing the fill within the context of a swing beat.

Track 60

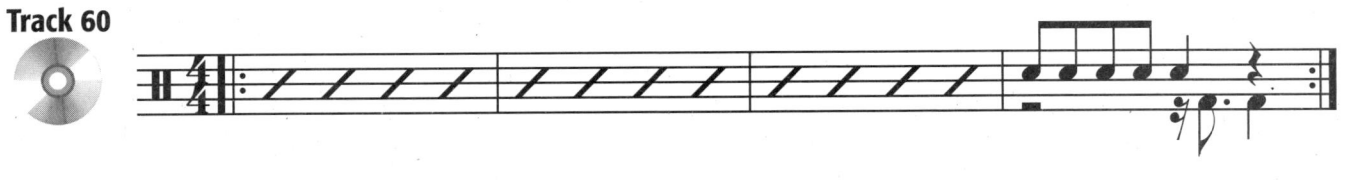

"Everybody Loves Somebody" (ex. 1)
FROM DEAN MARTIN'S *DREAM WITH DEAN* (1964)

Irv Cottler showcases some quick, yet delicate, left hand playing on the snare in this smooth drum fill. The three consecutive snare hits ending with the accent on beat 4 are a little tricky and take some practice to play smoothly, so start slowly, and gradually increase the tempo as you feel comfortable.

Original transcription (0:30):

Track 61

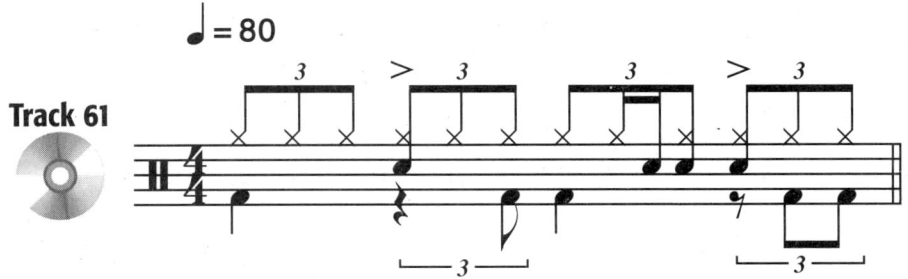

Now, try playing it within the context of the beat.

Track 62

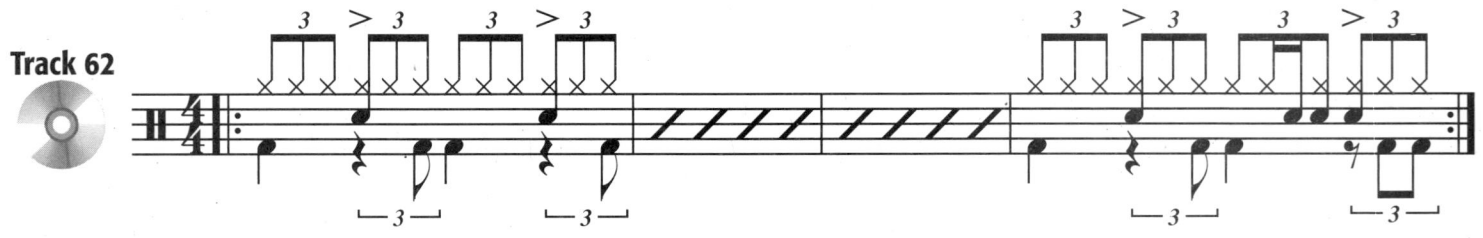

"Everybody Loves Somebody" (ex. 2)
FROM DEAN MARTIN'S *DREAM WITH DEAN* (1964)

Here's another beautiful drum fill played by Irv Cottler. In this excerpt, Cottler adds several snare hits throughout the drum fill while maintaining the continuity of the beat with the ride cymbal.

Original transcription (0:54):

Track 63

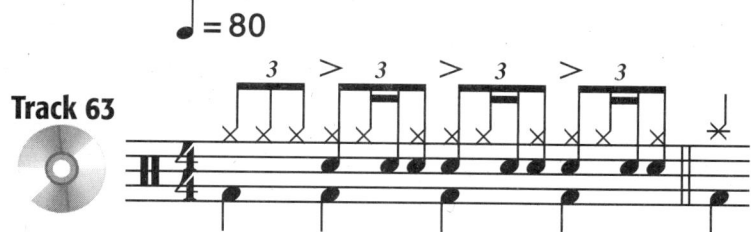

Let's start by playing and repeating this simplified version of the fill. Play triplets on the ride cymbal with your right hand, the snare drum on beats 2 and 4 with your left hand, and the kick on beats 1, 2, 3, and 4. Hit the snare with your left stick in the space between the second and third notes of the triplet that starts on beat 4, immediately followed by another snare hit with your left stick on the third note of the triplet. Go ahead and give it a try. Start slowly at first, and gradually increase the tempo as you feel comfortable.

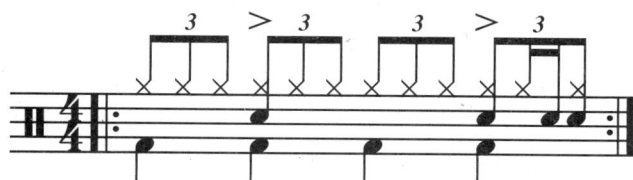

Next, let's add the same pattern starting on beat 2.

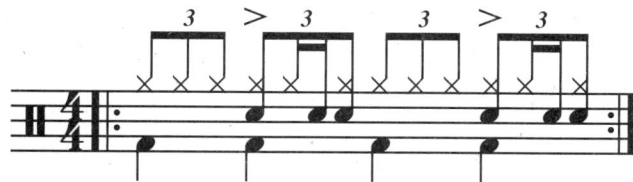

Finally, add the same pattern to beat 3, and with a little practice, you'll be playing the drum fill just like Irv Cottler plays it on the recording.

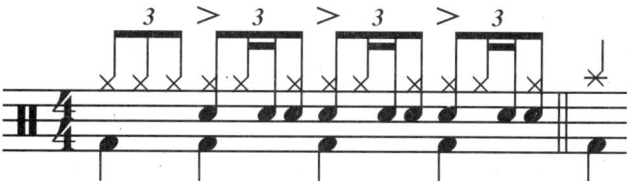

Congratulations!

You have completed **Level 2** of the *On the Beaten Path: Beginning Drumset Course.* **Level 3** explores **authentic** country, funk, reggae, and Latin beats, in addition to more authentic jazz beats and jazz fills. **Plus,** you'll learn about first and second endings, polyrhythms, sextuplets, dropping bombs, rim shots, open hi-hat splashes, stick clicks, the 5-stroke roll, trading fours, and buzz strokes. You'll also learn to play in more time signatures, and to play with time/meter/tempo manipulations like double time, half time, ritardandos, and accelerandos. So, what are you waiting for? Let's get started on **Level 3!**